Fantastic Recycled Plastic

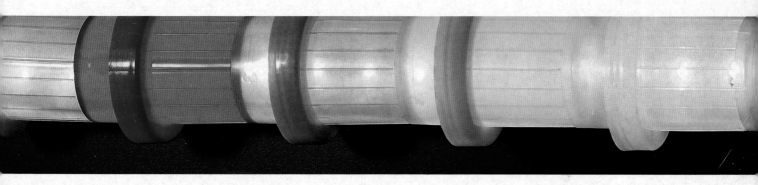

Fantastic Recycled Plastic

30 Clever Creations to Spark Your Imagination

David Edgar
Robin A. Edgar

LARK BOOKS

A Division of Sterling Publishing Co., Inc.
New York / London

Senior Editor: **Terry Taylor**

Production Editor: **Linda Kopp**

Assistant Editors:
Beth Sweet, Amanda Carestio

Art Director: **Kristi Pfeffer**

Illustrator: **Orrin Lundgren**

Photographer: **Steve Mann**

Cover Designer: **Eric Stevens**

Dedication:

To my parents, Allen and Joan Edgar, for their indulgent patience and dedicated support of my choice of an artistic career.

Library of Congress Cataloging-in-Publication Data

Edgar, David, 1953-
  Fantastic recycled plastic : 30 clever creations to spark your imagination / David Edgar and Robin Edgar. -- 1st ed.
      p. cm.
  Includes index.
  ISBN 978-1-60059-342-0 (pb-pbk. with flaps : alk. paper)
  1. Plastics craft. 2. Plastic scrap--Recycling. I. Edgar, Robin, 1951-
II. Title.
  TT297.E23 2009
  745.57'2--dc22

                                    2008050621

10 9 8 7 6 5 4 3 2 1

First Edition

Published by Lark Books, A Division of
Sterling Publishing Co., Inc.
387 Park Avenue South, New York, NY 10016

Text © 2009, David Edgar and Robin A. Edgar
Photography © 2009, Lark Books, a Division of Sterling Publishing Co., Inc.,
unless otherwise specified
Illustrations © 2009, Lark Books, a Division of Sterling Publishing Co., Inc.,
unless otherwise specified

Distributed in Canada by Sterling Publishing,
c/o Canadian Manda Group, 165 Dufferin Street
Toronto, Ontario, Canada M6K 3H6

Distributed in the United Kingdom by GMC Distribution Services,
Castle Place, 166 High Street, Lewes, East Sussex, England BN7 1XU

Distributed in Australia by Capricorn Link (Australia) Pty Ltd.,
P.O. Box 704, Windsor, NSW 2756 Australia

If you have questions or comments about this book, please contact:
Lark Books
67 Broadway
Asheville, NC 28801
828-253-0467

Manufactured in China

For information about custom editions, special sales, premium and corporate purchases, please contact Sterling Special Sales Department at 800-805-5489 or specialsales@sterlingpub.com.

 This book was printed on recycled paper with agri-based inks.

Contents

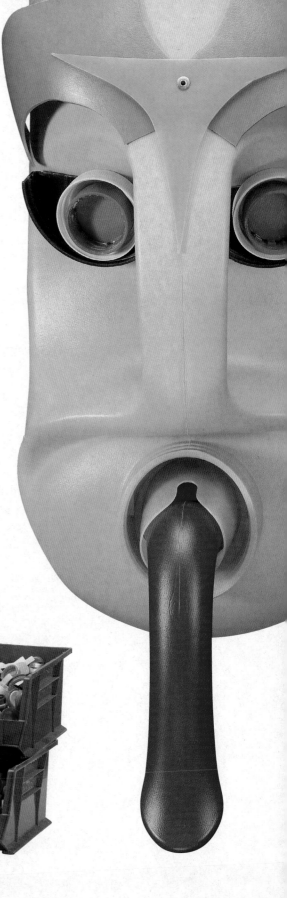

Projects

Decorative and Wearable Art

Dimensional Figures

Holiday Decorations

More Dimensional Figures

Toys

Lighting

Introduction
How I Got Started Working with Recycled Plastic

Like many kids growing up in the early 1960s, I rode my bicycle to school.
I often came home with my bike basket full of old radios or military and camping equipment. My mother complained that I was bringing home a bunch of junk, to which I replied, "Mom, this is all really great stuff," as I headed to the garage to disassemble my treasures. (I guess I was way ahead of my time as far as recycling and "living green.")

By the time I got to high school, I was making welded metal sculptures using found materials like cement nails and ball bearings. In college, I idolized American sculptors like David Smith and Alexander Calder, and I became familiar with the work of found-object artists like Joseph Cornell and the ready-made artworks of surrealists like Marcel Duchamp.

Over the next 30 years of working with fabricated steel, I began experimenting with a wide range of found-object "junque." All of this somehow led to my work in plastic, which began when I was invited to attend a Super Bowl party. Wanting to show team spirit, I grabbed an empty laundry detergent bottle that was just the right color and crafted a team mascot mask.

In no time at all, I was hooked. I found that the properties of plastic were surprisingly similar to metal. Both are refined earth elements—plastic is from oil and metal is from iron ore—that are molded and extruded from a liquid form.

I thought I was fooling myself about this new work until Lloyd Herman, who wrote the Afterword for this book, selected several of my pieces for an exhibit called Trashformations at the Fuller Craft Museum in Brockton, Massachusetts. That show, which traveled to three other national venues, convinced me that I was on to something. Since that time, my work has been exhibited internationally and is now included in a growing number of accredited museum collections.

Focusing initially on marine imagery, it dawned on me that pollutants spread from plastic containers could eventually mutate into what I now call Creatures from the Plastiquarium. This work is a social commentary on what consumer culture is doing to our ecology. Finding comparatively few people working in this medium, I have made a conscious effort to introduce others to the potential of making art from recycled plastics through my exhibitions and workshops. I hope this book will inspire you to do so as well!

DAVID EDGAR

A Handmade World, 2009

66 x 66 inches (1.7 m x 1.7 m) Plastic hand silhouettes

Collection of The Creative Discovery Museum,
Chattanooga, Tennessee

Photo by Alex McMahan

Plastics
Today's Disposable Packaging

The History of Plastic

Plastic has been around for a long time in the form of natural polymers such as amber, tortoiseshells, and animal horns. Resins found in some trees and plants also have certain plastic-like characteristics. These natural polymers were used for the original horn-rimmed glasses and tortoiseshell combs, because the material could be heated and molded into the desired shapes, just like plastic.

The human-made version, however, was not formally introduced until 1862 at the London International Exhibition on Industry and Art. Using organic material derived from cellulose (plant fiber), Alexander Parkes dubbed his invention Parkesine and claimed it had the same qualities of rubber but was less expensive to produce.

The history of plastics is filled with accidental spills. The first true thermoplastic, which is the formal name for what we commonly think of as plastic, was discovered quite by accident, when American photographer John Wesley Hyatt noticed that some collodion, a nitrocellulose compound used to make photographic plates, had spilled on his desk and congealed into a tough, flexible film. When he added camphor, Hyatt found that the substance retained its shape after being molded under heat and pressure, and he used it to make thermoplastic billiard balls, saving many an elephant. (With the popular parlor game of billiards on the rise in the late 1800s, massive amounts of ivory were being acquired at the expense of thousands of elephants.) Hyatt later created celluloid, so we also have him to thank for the film that made those great early motion pictures possible.

Plastic Recycling Facts

In 1907, New York chemist Leo Hendrik Baekeland coined the term plastics for the synthetic polymer made from coal tar that he called Bakelite. Used for high-tech objects including cameras and telephones, it also became popular for housewares and jewelry items.

Once again, an accidental spill led to a discovery. This time, wine on a tablecloth prompted Swiss textile engineer Dr. Jacques Edwin Brandenberger to develop viscose in 1913. Brandenberger was hoping to develop a waterproof coating for fabric to prevent staining, but he ultimately found viscose too brittle for that purpose. However, it later became useful as the clear and flexible-membrane packaging known today as cellophane.

During the plastics craze of the 1920s, the human-made substance served as a less-expensive substitute for wood, glass, and metal. Manufacturers found it cheaper to make plastics from petroleum than from coal tar and, as a result, many different types of plastics were created. Wallace Hume Carothers of DuPont developed nylon (known at the time as Fiber 66), Waldo Semon at B.F. Goodrich created polyvinyl chloride (PVC), and Ralph Wiley of Dow Chemical discovered polyvinylidene chloride (saran).

Another accidental spill, this time at the Imperial Chemical Industries Research Laboratory, led researchers E.W. Fawcett and R.O. Gibson to discover polyethylene. When a test tube containing ethylene and benzaldehyde sprang a leak, they found that the resulting white, waxy substance resembling plastic was a good electrical insulator. By the time World War II began, it was being used to coat and insulate underwater cable. The most widely used plastic in the world today, polyethylene is found in common consumer items such as soda bottles, milk jugs, and other grocery and food-storage containers.

With plastic so omnipresent, it is hard to conceive of a time when it was not around. After all, who among us doesn't pay with plastic?

Plastic has taken over our world. To prove it, let's go on a treasure hunt and count how many plastic objects you can find in your kitchen. Look in the refrigerator, probably made with plastic walls and shelves, and count the plastic containers. Now, add the small appliances (don't forget the TV remote). There are probably PVC pipes under the sink and perhaps plastic laminate countertops. Did you count the plastic wrap and bags in your drawers?

Unfortunately, plastic is not biodegradable, and very little of it (less than 4 percent) is recycled. Approximately 63 pounds (28.6 kg) of plastic packaging per person per year goes into U.S. landfills, including eight out of 10 plastic water bottles, which take 700 years before they even begin to decompose. If the caps are not removed, the bottles cannot be compressed. A 63-pound (28.6 kg) pile of plastic bottles looks something like what you see in the photo below.

And that's not all. Preproduction plastic pellets, lost during industrial processing, make up 10 percent of the debris found on beaches; there are also the plastic sunglasses, sand toys, and bottles left behind. Even worse, about 46,000 pieces of plastic float in each square mile of our oceans.

Here I am with a 63 lb (28.6 kg) pile of plastic.

Great Pacific Garbage Patch

Referred to by oceanographers as the Great Pacific Garbage Patch, the North Pacific Central Gyre is one of five high-atmospheric-pressure zones in the oceans created by a mass of air heated at the equator that travels in a gentle clockwise rotation. Forty percent of the oceans are classified as subtropical gyres, making a fourth of the planet's surface area the accumulator of floating plastic debris!

Whatever washes from our rivers into the sea may eventually wind up in this swirling vortex about the size of Texas. Scientists estimate that for every pound (.45 kg) of naturally occurring zooplankton in the North Pacific's subtropical gyre, there are six pounds (2.7 kg) of plastic. Sea creatures, many of them endangered, mistake colorful plastic pieces floating on the ocean's surface for food. This leads to malnutrition, dehydration, and eventually death. Scientists estimate that plastic kills up to one million sea birds, 100,000 sea mammals, and countless fish each year.

What's more, plastic adsorbs hydrophobic pollutants, like PCBs, and pesticides, like DDT. These endocrine disruptors cause reproductive problems in animals and accumulate in the tissues of marine organisms, eventually finding their way up the food chain into the foods that we humans eat.

Taken on Green Island, Kure Atoll, on July 13, 2004, David Liittschwager's photograph of a Laysan Albatross and Susan Middleton's photograph of its stomach contents (over ¾ pound [.3 kg] of plastic and other indigestible material) show the tragic effect of plastic debris found in the North Pacific's subtropical gyre.

Nearly 80 percent of marine debris comes from land-based sources, conveyed mostly as urban runoff through storm drains. The main sources of plastic and other types of anthropogenic (human-made) debris include litter (mostly bags, packaging, and single-use disposable products), industrial discharges, garbage transportation, landfills, construction debris, and detritus from commercial establishments and public venues. The good news is that more and more people are reusing plastic bottles or recycling their plastic consumer products, either in curbside neighborhood bins or through their art— like us! Hundreds of companies are also finding ways to use recyclable material to manufacture goods such as apparel and backpacks, funnels and ice scrapers, trash cans and liners, dumpsters, insulation, shingles, carpet and geotextile fiber (a permeable fabric used in landscaping), sheds and feed carts, blankets and hammocks, decking and fencing, paper clips, key chains, cameras, sandboxes, signs, and more.

View of a local recycling center

100 percent recycled plastic Adirondack Rocking Chair
Photo provided by Barco Products, www.barcoproducts.com

100 percent recycled plastic colanders
Photo provided by Recycline, Inc.

Local Recycling

In part, the highly visible curbside recycling program where I live inspires my Plastiquarium artwork. Every morning, my wife, Robin, and I walk a two-mile circuit in our neighborhood and, on recycling day, the interesting shapes and colors of cast-off plastic containers in the recycling bins trigger my hunter-gatherer instincts for found objects. With stringer in hand, we troll for the best catches of the week.

When I received a grant to partner with the local recycling center to conduct public education workshops and demonstrate my art, I became increasingly impressed with the scope of how Mecklenburg County, North Carolina's recycling program addresses this important environmental topic. Each week, they collect cardboard, paper, glass, metal, and plastic (my favorite) that residents place in bins by the curb. A driver comes by in a special truck and separates this material into two groups while picking it up: the first group is cardboard and paper, and the second is glass, metal, and plastic.

At the recycling center, the fiber-based cardboard and paper are processed directly on-site by an insulation-manufacturing company to make bulk cellulose for blown-in insulation for the construction industry. This is a great way to conserve transportation energy costs: the company makes a recycled product which, in turn, conserves heating and cooling energy! The other assorted items collected from the neighborhood recycling bins are sorted by type and baled for sale and shipment to recycled-materials processing companies around the country.

All of this helps to fund the county recycling program, which is completely self-funded. Just to give you an idea, in the fiscal year from 2007 to 2008, the county collected 59,000 tons of recyclables that resulted in about $7 million in sales of bulk recyclable materials. This included $1.5 million (over 20 percent) in recyclable plastics. It appears that well-run government recycling programs do not require out-of-pocket expenses for the taxpayers. You may want to learn more about how your local officials handle these issues in your neck of the woods.

One interesting note: In recent years, U.S. manufacturing companies that use recyclable cardboard and paper are being outbid by Asian companies for these raw materials. Interestingly, this has started to happen with the sale of bulk recyclable plastics as well. The effect of internationalizing the market for recyclable materials is driving prices for the bulk material higher. These prices will also increase with the rising cost of the oil used to make plastic.

Domestic Recycled HDPE Bottle End Use

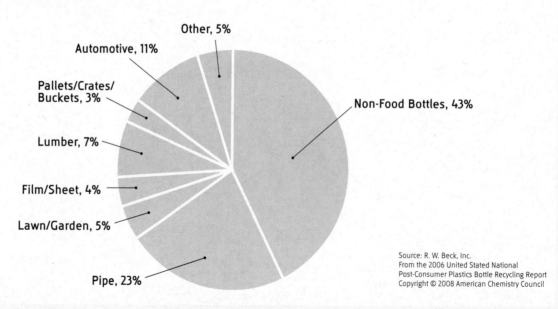

- Other, 5%
- Automotive, 11%
- Pallets/Crates/Buckets, 3%
- Lumber, 7%
- Film/Sheet, 4%
- Lawn/Garden, 5%
- Pipe, 23%
- Non-Food Bottles, 43%

Source: R. W. Beck, Inc.
From the 2006 United Stated National
Post-Consumer Plastics Bottle Recycling Report
Copyright © 2008 American Chemistry Council

Characteristics and Properties of Plastic

Polymers abound in nature. Even deoxyribonucleic acid (DNA), the long chain of molecules that represents the blueprint for all living things, is a polymer. Spider silk, hair, and horn are protein polymers. Starch can be a polymer, as is cellulose in wood. Rubber-tree latex and cellulose have been used as raw material to make organic rubber and plastics. The majority of manufactured plastics are derived from petrochemicals such as coal tar, petroleum, and natural gas. When these are manufactured, they need to be recycled because they do not biodegrade.

Plastics fall into two categories: thermoplastic (sometimes called thermoforming) and thermosetting. The primary difference between the two is their behavior when heated. Thermoforming plastics, used to make detergent and beverage bottles, constitute all of the conventionally recyclable plastics and can be heated and reshaped repeatedly. Thermosetting plastics, such as fiberglass resins used to make items like modular shower stalls and surfboards, cannot be heated and reformed, which limits their ability to be recycled.

Recycle number one (PETE) and recycle number two (HDPE) are both thermoforming (see pages 16–17 for information about the universal recycling category symbols). Virtually any plastic container will have a recycling category symbol marked on the bottom.

In the cooled or solid state, HDPE and PETE plastics have a memory, so even after they are cut and twisted they will tend to return to their original shapes unless reheated. HDPE softens and melts at a comparatively low temperature, making it possible to use a heat gun or even an ordinary hair dryer to soften and re-form the contours to a new shape. This type of plastic is usually used for common household containers such as detergent bottles. PETE, on the other hand, is not easily controlled and manipulated to retain a new shape once reheated. Rather than reshaping, its former shape will twist and contort; it tends to contract toward the heat source.

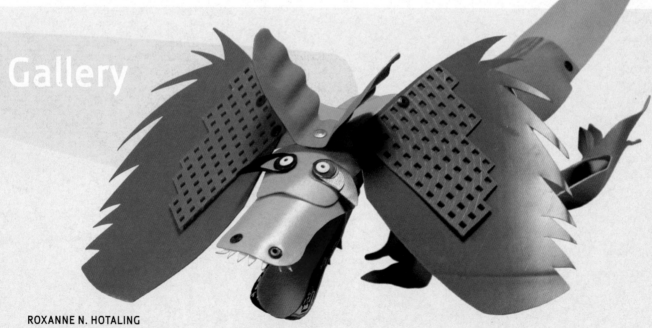

Gallery

ROXANNE N. HOTALING
Recycled Dilophosaurus Turquoise, 2008
5 x 10 x 21 inches (12.7 x 25.4 x 53.3 cm)
Recycled plastic; heat shaped, riveted
Photo by Steve Loar

Plastic Packaging Resins Identification Chart

RESIN CODES	DESCRIPTIONS	PROPERTIES	PRODUCT APPLICATIONS	PRODUCTS MADE WITH RECYCLED CONTENT
1 PET	**Polyethylene Terephthalate (PET, PETE).** PET is clear, tough, and has good gas and moisture barrier properties. This resin is commonly used in beverage bottles and many injection-molded consumer product containers. Cleaned, recycled PET flakes and pellets are in great demand for spinning fiber for carpet yarns, producing fiberfill and geotextiles. Nickname: Polyester.	• Clear and optically smooth surfaces for oriented films and bottles • Excellent barrier to oxygen, water, and carbon dioxide • High impact capability and shatter resistance • Excellent resistance to most solvents • Capability for hotfilling	Plastic bottles for soft drinks, water, juice, sports drinks, beer, mouthwash, catsup and salad dressing. Food jars for peanut butter, jelly, jam and pickles. Ovenable film and microwavable food trays. In addition to packaging, PET's major uses are textiles, monofilament, carpet, strapping, films, and engineering moldings.	Fiber for carpet, fleece jackets, comforter fill, and tote bags. Containers for food, beverages (bottles), and non-food items. Film and sheet. Strapping.
2 HDPE	**High Density Polyethylene (HDPE).** HDPE is used to make many types of bottles. Unpigmented bottles are translucent, have good barrier properties and stiffness, and are well suited to packaging products with a short shelf life such as milk. Because HDPE has good chemical resistance, it is used for packaging many household and industrial chemicals such as detergents and bleach. Pigmented HDPE bottles have better stress crack resistance than unpigmented HDPE.	• Excellent resistance to most solvents • Higher tensile strength compared to other forms of polyethylene • Relatively stiff material with useful temperature capabilities	Bottles for milk, water, juice, cosmetics, shampoo, dish and laundry detergents, and household cleaners. Bags for groceries and retail purchases. Cereal box liners. Reusable shipping containers. In addition to packaging, HDPE's major uses are in injection molding applications, extruded pipe and conduit, plastic wood composites, and wire and cable covering.	Bottles for non-food items, such as shampoo, conditioner, liquid laundry detergent, household cleaners, motor oil and antifreeze. Plastic lumber for outdoor decking, fencing and picnic tables. Pipe, floor tiles, buckets, crates, flower pots, garden edging, film and sheet, and recycling bins.
4 LDPE	**Low Density Polyethylene (LDPE).** LDPE is used predominately in film applications due to its toughness, flexibility and relative transparency, making it popular for use in applications where heat sealing is necessary. LDPE also is used to manufacture some flexible lids and bottles as well as in wire and cable applications. Includes Linear Low Density Polyethylene (LLDPE).	• Excellent resistance to acids, bases and vegetable oils • Toughness, flexibility and relative transparency (good combination of properties for packaging applications requiring heat-sealing)	Bags for dry cleaning, newspapers, bread, frozen foods, fresh produce, and household garbage. Shrink wrap and stretch film. Coatings for paper milk cartons and hot and cold beverage cups. Container lids. Toys. Squeezable bottles (e.g., honey and mustard). In addition to packaging, LDPE's major uses are in injection molding applications, adhesives and sealants, and wire and cable coverings.	Shipping envelopes, garbage can liners, floor tile, paneling, furniture, film and sheet, compost bins, trash cans, landscape timber, and outdoor lumber.

RESIN CODES	DESCRIPTIONS	PROPERTIES	PRODUCT APPLICATIONS	PRODUCTS MADE WITH RECYCLED CONTENT
6 PS	**Polystyrene (PS).** PS is a versatile plastic that can be rigid or foamed. General purpose polystyrene is clear, hard and brittle. It has a relatively low melting point. Typical applications include protective packaging, foodservice packaging, bottles, and food containers. PS is often combined with rubber to make high impact polystyrene (HIPS) which is used for packaging and durable applications requiring toughness, but not clarity.	• Excellent moisture barrier for short shelf life products • Excellent optical clarity in general purpose form • Significant stiffness in both foamed and rigid forms. • Low density and high stiffness in foamed applications • Low thermal conductivity and excellent insulation properties in foamed form	Food service items, such as cups, plates, bowls, cutlery, hinged takeout containers (clamshells), meat and poultry trays, and rigid food containers (e.g., yogurt). These items may be made with foamed or non-foamed PS. Protective foam packaging for furniture, electronics and other delicate items. Packing peanuts, known as "loose fill." Compact disc cases and aspirin bottles. In addition to packaging, PS's major uses are in agricultural trays, electronic housings, cable spools, building insulation, video cassette cartridges, coat hangers, and medical products and toys.	Thermal insulation, thermometers, light switch plates, vents, desk trays, rulers, and license plate frames. Cameras or video cassette casings. Foamed foodservice applications, such as egg shell cartons. Plastic mouldings (i.e., wood replacement products). Expandable polystyrene (EPS) foam protective packaging.
7 OTHER	**Other.** Use of this code indicates that a package is made with a resin other than the six listed above, or is made of more than one resin and used in a multi-layer combination.	Dependent on resin or combination of resins	Three- and five-gallon reusable water bottles, some citrus juice and catsup bottles. Oven-baking bags, barrier layers, and custom packaging.	Bottles and plastic lumber applications.

Gallery

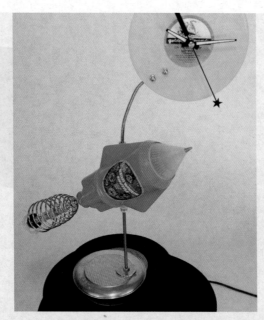

GREG STANGE

P-F-F (poof) Rocket, 2007

25 x 12½ x 12½ inches (63.5 x 31.8 x 31.8 cm)Records, plastic toys, wooden game tiles, wood bead, record insert, egg holder, aluminum plate, glass light cover, clock mechanism and hand, night light assembly, nuts, bolts, washers; assembled, drilled

Photo by artist

Safety Precautions for Working with Recycled Plastic

General Precautions

Working with recyclable plastics has only one hard-and-fast rule: Never heat the plastic to the point of incineration, as the actual burning of the plastic may give off toxic gases. Gloves are a necessity for safely handling heated plastic. I recommend synthetic leather gloves. Be sure to work in a well-ventilated area when you heat plastics.

Collecting Recycled Plastic

When collecting recycled plastics, you should always read the label on the container to learn what the contents were/are and the recommended safe-handling precautions. You should also be aware that the previous owner may have used an empty container to store or discard a product with harsher or perhaps even more dangerous ingredients. Some containers to avoid or use with caution are those that stored products such as drain cleaner, antifreeze, and pesticides. I also avoid using oil containers of any type whenever possible due to the inconvenience of trying to get them clean. All containers should be rinsed and cleaned thoroughly before you repurpose them for your art (see section on preparation of materials on page 27).

Cutting Plastic Containers

Sharp tools are your friends and dull tools are your enemies. Plastic edges can be very sharp, and sharp points can result in a healthy poke in the eye. I recommend wearing protective glasses and close-fitting work gloves to protect you from harm. Only use craft and utility knives with razor-blade edges.

General Precautions

Due to the rigorous nature of cutting and heating plastics, children under the age of 13 should have adult supervision at all times. It's always a good idea to keep a well-stocked first-aid kit in the studio area. Sharp objects cut professionals as well as novices!

Tools and Materials for Working with Plastic

You can usually find most of what you need for working with plastics in your kitchen drawers or garage workshop. The suggested tools and equipment are fairly inexpensive and can also be found at most builders' supply or hardware stores unless otherwise noted.

Cutting Tools

Knives

A sturdy razor-blade utility knife is a basic part of a tool kit when working with plastics. Since it is difficult to control and does not always cut accurately, a utility knife is usually used for rough-in tasks like cutting the spouts off of bottles, refining edges, and removing burrs left by another cutting tool, such as a band saw.

A pencil-point-tipped craft knife is easier to control than a utility knife. It is very helpful for cleaning burrs out of drilled holes as well as for other clean-up detailing.

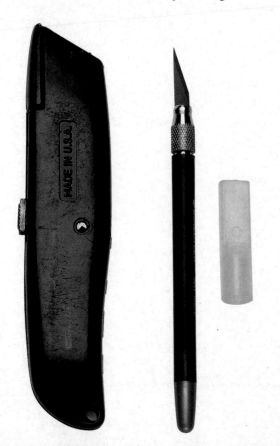

Scissors and Shears

A good pair of high-quality, sharp utility scissors is the best all-around tool for cutting recycled plastics. It is good to have three different sizes: one for general cutting, one for heavier material, and one for detail work. You can purchase good scissors at craft, hardware, and kitchen-supply stores. Look for large, cushioned handles and short blades, which will serve you better than long blades and small handles. Make sure that the tips cross at the end so you can achieve a clean edge at the end of a cut. Some types of scissors have a slightly serrated edge along the cutting surface, which is very helpful for gripping the material to make accurate cuts like shaving the outside edge of a shape.

Pinking shears are also useful to have in your tool kit. They make great decorative edges. The decorative-edge-bordering scissors made for scrapbooking that have plastic frames are not sturdy enough to cut plastics.

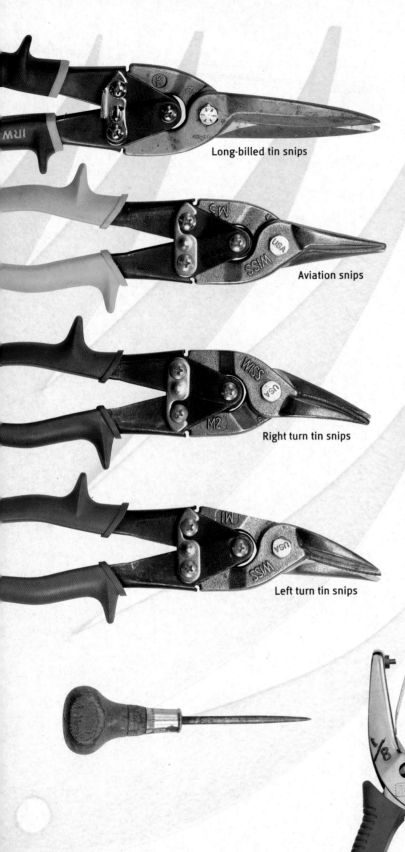

Snips

Tin snips, sometimes called aviation snips, are excellent for cutting recycled plastics, particularly thicker material. Most manufacturers make at least three formats of tin snips. Those with yellow handles are for general-purpose cutting. I have found the long-billed, straight-cutting tin snips to be helpful for doing rough-in work. More importantly, for making concave cuts that are on the inside of a curve, you should invest in two quality pairs of tin snips: green handled for right-turn cutting, and red handled for left-turn cutting. Once you acquire your tin snips, avoid using them for cutting metal, as they will quickly become too dull to use on recycled plastic.

Awl

A sharp awl is excellent for getting holes started where you plan to drill. It also transfers markings through several layers of material.

Punches

There is an extensive variety of hole punches in the scrapbooking section of your local craft and hobby shop. Be sure to select the type with a full metal frame, because those with plastic frames do not stand up to the rigors of working with plastic. Note: Even a metal-framed punch will not work on thicker parts of plastic containers. The ⅛-inch (3 mm) round punch is the most utilitarian to have, but you may also want to have a series of sizes and shapes for decorative details.

Long-billed tin snips

Aviation snips

Right turn tin snips

Left turn tin snips

Forming Tools

Cardboard

Keep a few sheets of stiff, noncorrugated cardboard, also known as poster board, on hand to make patterns of designs that you want to replicate. Cardboard from an old cereal box or priority mail envelope works just fine for this. You can also use patterns to make matching sides (mirror images). While some basic patterns are included in this book, the more advanced crafters will develop their own patterns over time.

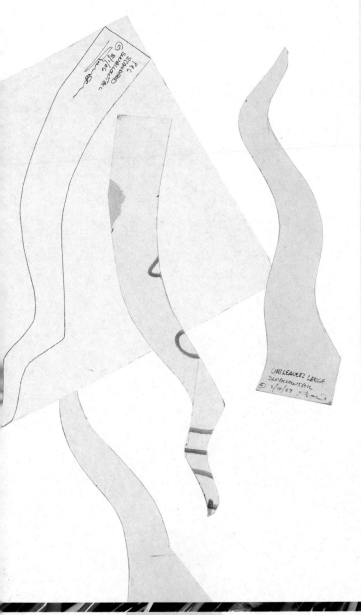

JOHN D. RICHARDS
Wire Man, 2006
23 x 15 x 9 inches (58.4 x 38.1 x 22.9 cm)
Iron, brass, copper, aluminum wire, polystyrene trash; twisted
Photo by Tom Mills

Gallery

Pliers

Any pair of needle-nose pliers can be used to bend or fold heated plastic. You can also use duck-billed sheet metal pliers for this purpose. Pliers are also used for other miscellaneous tasks, such as folding over staple points and bending wire to hang your finished product.

Curling Iron

The more advanced crafter may want to experiment with an electric curling iron as a shaping tool.

Heat Gun

The heat gun is the recycled-plastic crafter's basic forming tool to soften the plastic in order to manipulate it into different configurations. Note: It is important to use heat-tolerant gloves when using this tool. Some heat guns are sold specifically for paint stripping and frequently come with an assortment of nozzles that control the stream of hot air. Be sure to acquire one that has a base that allows you to stand the gun, nozzle-end up, on your worktable for hands-free operation. Beginners can also use an ordinary hair dryer.

Blower Fan

Although not required, a fan is helpful to rapidly cool heated plastic in order to set the new shape created by the previously mentioned forming tools. A blower-type fan with a focused stream of air works best.

Fastening Tools

Nut Driver

You will need a ⁵⁄₁₆-inch (8 mm) nut driver to tighten the matching nuts for the #6-32 machine screws recommended to hold the various parts of your recycled plastic work together.

Screwdrivers and Machine Screws

I recommend using #6-32 machine screws to fasten the layers of your crafted recycled art. Ordinary flat-head and Phillips screwdrivers are necessary to tighten the machine screws once you have applied the nuts. A very small screwdriver used for electronic tasks is also helpful for working in tight spaces, like inside a bottle cap.

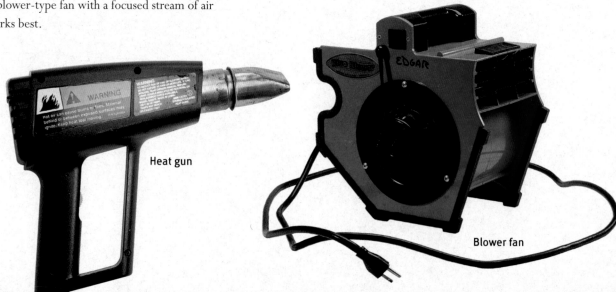

Heat gun

Blower fan

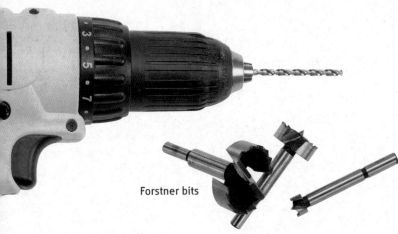

Forstner bits

Compression Block

A small piece of wood, about 4 inches (10.2 cm) square and ½ inch (1.3 cm) thick, with a few ¼-inch (6 mm) holes drilled all the way through it, is used to compress small assemblies of plastic between the backing washer and the flaring of a pop rivet.

Pop Rivets and Pop Rivet Gun

A more elegant alternative to using a machine screw is a ⅛-inch (3 mm) button-head pop rivet (also known as a blind rivet). You will also need backing washers that fit this size pop rivet. For setting these rivets, you will need a hand-operated pop rivet gun.

Electric Staple Gun and Staples

An electric staple gun with ½-inch (1.3 cm) staples will quickly fasten pieces where the fastening point (staple) can be hidden by a subsequent layer.

Glue Gun

Hot glue is helpful for a variety of applications, such as securing a colored liner inside a bottle cap for an eye. Any hot glue gun will suffice for this task (see safety precautions). Note: Hot glue is not reliable for attaching one flat surface to another flat surface.

Drills and Bits

A light-duty, cordless drill is an everyday workbench staple when working with plastics. I recommend using ⅛-inch (3 mm) light-duty fasteners such as #6-32 machine screws and ⅛-inch (3 mm) pop rivets to hold the various parts of your recycled plastic work together. Use a new (sharp!) ⁵⁄₃₂-inch (4 mm) drill bit (the next size larger than ⅛ inch [3 mm]) for making the correct-sized hole. More advanced artists may also want to acquire a set of Forstner bits for drilling larger holes.

Staple and Drilling Pad

A couple of small pieces of ½-inch-thick (1.3 cm), three-ply corrugated cardboard like the kind you can find at a piano store will protect your workbench surface when you are drilling or stapling. If you don't have access to a piano store, you can tape together three pieces of corrugated cardboard to make the pad. Make sure the pad is at least ½ inch (1.3 cm) thick.

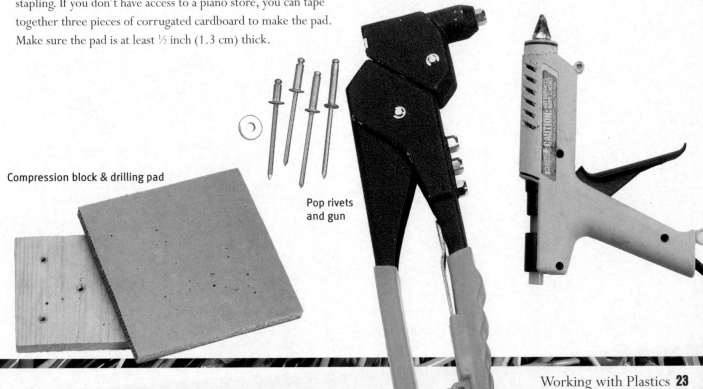

Compression block & drilling pad

Pop rivets and gun

Masking Tape

Masking tape holds pieces in alignment when you are drilling or cutting.

Gloves

Close-fitting, heat-tolerant gloves are essential when you are handling hot plastic (see safety precautions on page 18).

Marker

A fine-point permanent marker is useful for marking locations, tracing outlines, and signing your work. A dry-erase marker is also helpful to mark cutting lines, which can then easily be removed when done.

Pin Backs

Pin backs, with and without adhesive strips, are available in several sizes at local craft and hobby shops. These are used for wearable art items, such as the Piscatorial Pins (page 34).

Magnets

Magnets, with and without adhesive strips, are available in several sizes at local craft and hobby shops. These are used for small, decorative display projects, such as the Colorful Canines (page 36) or the Sci-Fi Comet (page 38).

Copper Wire

Medium (12-gauge) copper or steel wire is good to keep on hand for hanging your completed pieces. Scrap pieces of light (14-gauge) and heavy (10-gauge) copper or steel wire may also be used.

Monofilament Line

Fishing line or another type of thin but durable stringing material is used in projects such as the Boa Necklace (page 44) and the Festive Garland (page 76).

Rotary Tool

A small rotary tool with an abrasive wheel will roughen a smooth surface in preparation for gluing.

Squeeze Clamps

Several small squeeze clamps hold pieces in alignment while tracing, cutting, or fastening.

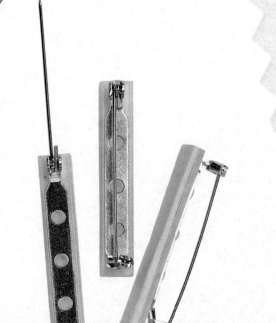

Nylon Scrubbing Pad

A nylon pad, typically used for scrubbing kitchen pots, removes date stamps, stains, glue, and visible marker lines on containers without scratching the surfaces.

Metal File

A metal file rounds off sharp ends of machine screws that may stick out of the backs of your projects.

Hammer

An ordinary household hammer tightens and flattens folded-over staples.

Trays

A few simple plastic cafeteria-style trays are helpful to work over for catching scraps and to transport your projects and tools.

Lamp

Use a swing-arm or any small lamp to lluminate your workspace. Good lighting is important.

Bins

Old shoeboxes are excellent for sorting scrap materials by size, color, etc. However, the translucent plastic bins found in hobby shops or office supply stores work the best.

Telescoping Magnet on a Stick

When fastening a whole bottle onto a larger project, a telescoping magnet enables you to maneuver a steel fastener component in place.

Electrical Crimping Tool with Stud Cutter and Wire Strippers

This tool is used for stripping the insulation off of copper wire and for cutting machine screws and all-thread (threaded rod) into specific lengths.

Hacksaw

Use a hacksaw to cut thick, rigid pieces of plastic like bottle caps and jar lids.

Band Saw

Although it is not required for working with plastic, a band saw can be helpful for cutting lids in half or making symmetrical cuts through whole bottles. The downside of using a band saw is that it leaves a feathery burr on the edge of the cut, but you can easily remove that with a craft or utility knife.

Electrical crimping tool

Anatomy of the Bottle

Thickness of the Walls

Most recyclable plastic bottles are made by blow molding. A thick-walled tube of heat-softened plastic is inserted into a two-part mold. As the mold closes around the tube, the tube is inflated (blown-up) to meet the contours of the mold. The plastic-lined mold is chilled, and the finished container is ejected. The thinner parts are usually the sides; the neck and bottom of the container are generally thicker and harder to cut.

Spouts

Manufacturers use a variety of ways to attach the pouring spout to a bottle. Some spouts are hot-glued in place, others are heat-welded, and many are compression-fitted. The compression-fitted type is easily pulled out; the others have to be cut off.

Labels

Some HDPE plastic manufacturers actually print labels directly on the container, making them virtually impossible to remove. Most labels are heat-laminated, and can be removed only with limited success by heating the bottle to soften the glue until it relaxes enough to peel off the label. Some labels are affixed with a petroleum-based adhesive and can easily be peeled off. I prefer to use a citrus-based solvents to remove any remaining adhesive.

Labels are often printed directly on PETE containers, and I have yet to figure out how to remove them. Some manufacturers print the labels on a clear film, which can be peeled away. The labels for most PETE soda bottles and HDPE bleach bottles wrap around and are only glued at each end. Shrink-wrapped labels are found on both HDPE and PETE bottles

Handles

PETE and HDPE bottle handles may be thick- or thin-walled, depending on the shape of the mold. You'll find unique shapes to inspire you when deconstructing this part of the bottle.

Necks

Most HDPE and PETE bottles come with threaded necks for screw-on caps. The threads, in conjunction with a matching cap, often serve as a good way to attach components.

Caps

Screw-off caps come in numerous sizes, shapes, and colors and are especially handy for making eyes.

Nomenclature

I developed some names for the various parts of the basic detergent bottle. I'll refer to these parts in the project directions. Use the diagram below to familiarize yourself with the names and refer to it when following the project instructions, if needed.

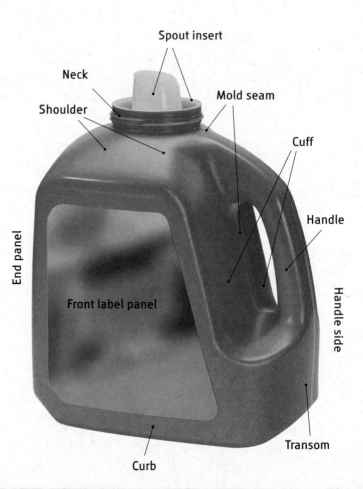

Deconstructing Techniques

Preparation of Materials

Drain any product residue and dispose of it appropriately. Rinse empty containers repeatedly with water until suds dissipate. Use white vinegar as the final rinse to reduce any remaining fragrance, and flush with water.

Before you get started, drain. Remove all of the lids from the bottles and pull out any removable pouring-spout inserts. The compression-fit spouts (usually white) are easy to remove and can be pulled out by wiggling and pulling them at the same time. You may need to grasp them with pliers. Spouts can be recycled or saved for use in various projects. Certain styles of spout inserts are not removable and will need to be cut off in a later step.

Removing Spouts

To carefully cut off any attached pouring spouts, use a utility knife to make an approximately 2-inch (5 cm) slit along the neck of the bottle, parallel with the edge of the spout (a). Note: A sawing motion works the best. Next, forcefully insert the lower blade of a pair of right-cutting tin snips (green-handled) into the slit and cut clockwise around the spout to remove it (b).

Rough-Cutting for Smaller Parts and Assembly Projects

Using long-bladed tin snips, (c) cut down along one side of the cuff, all the way to the curb of the container, and then continue to cut around the bottom to remove it. Make a second vertical cut along the other side of the cuff and remove the handle-side of the bottle. These pieces can be recycled or saved for future projects, since container bottoms are usually too thick and the handle shape is too difficult to work with for smaller assembly projects.

At this point, the front and back label panels of the bottle are connected by the end panel. There is also additional material along the edges where the handle was previously located, as well as along the shoulder where the pouring spout was removed. Using tin snips, remove any overly thick remaining material found along the shoulder area. These thick sections are difficult to use and can be recycled or saved for future projects.

In order to obtain a reasonably flat section of material to create smaller projects, cut along the vertical edges that connect the panels of the bottle (c). Cut desired shapes for projects starting from the edges rather than the center to conserve material.

Fastening Techniques

Pop Rivets

These wonderful mechanical fasteners elegantly attach multiple layers. Aluminum pop rivets are sufficient for working with plastic, which is not as rigid as other material, like metal. You will need to use backing washers to keep the pop rivets from pulling through.

When using only one pop rivet to attach several pieces together, the rivet must be very tight or the pieces will tend to rotate around the rivet like the hands of a clock. In order to make a tight rivet connection, use a compression block (see page 23) and make sure that the assembly fits snugly together and at least a little of the rivet is out beyond the backing washer. Push the stubby end of the rivet down into the compression block hole, and press down on the top of the pop rivet gun to tighten the whole assembly while you pop the rivet. Using this technique allows you to compress the assembly together and help snug the fastening.

Staples

Staples quickly attach one layer of plastic to another. Whenever possible, staple against your drilling pad (cardboard block) to allow the staple to penetrate all the way though the material. Once this is done, pull the assembly away from the cardboard and bend the points over from behind with a pair of needle-nose pliers. In certain circumstances, particularly involving thicker PETE plastic, the staples will not penetrate unless you warm the plastic with a heat gun.

Machine Screws

I often use #6-32 machine screws with matching washers and nuts. Use these miniature nuts and bolts to sandwich together as many layers of plastic as you can (see photos d–g). The ability to unfasten the machine screw to disassemble your work enables you to switch colors or shapes as needed. Use a $\frac{5}{32}$-inch (4 mm) drill bit to make the correct-sized hole for #6-32 screws. I suggest that you keep a selection of various lengths of screws, from $\frac{1}{2}$ inch (1.3 cm) to 2 inches (5 cm) or more, on hand.

A stick of several feet of continuously threaded machine screw material called all-thread, sometimes called threaded rod, can be purchased in most hardware stores. A piece of #6-32 all-thread can be cut with a stud cutter into the desired lengths for threading larger assemblies together.

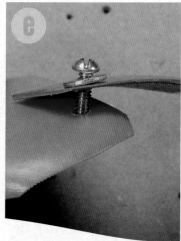

Glue

Gluing plastic can be a challenge because the human-made material is not very porous. For that reason, you should always score or roughen the surface to be glued. Entrapment gluing, where you fill up the space around a piece (for example, if you want to adhere spikes to the inside of a screw cap), is always preferable to gluing two flat surfaces together. I find that foaming and silicone-type glues work best for this.

Locking Tabs

You can employ a locking-tab technique to attach two pieces together. To do this, cut a triangular tab, approximately ⅝ inch (1.6 cm) long with a ⅜-inch-wide (9.5 mm) base, at the end of one of the pieces (h). At the base of this triangle, use a slotted punch to make two ⅛-inch-deep (3 mm) notches to create an arrowhead-shaped tab (i). To align these notches to where you want the tab to attach to the other piece, use the slotted punch to make an approximately ¼ x ⅛-inch (6 x 3 mm) rectangular-shaped slot (j). Slip the end of the tab into the slot and pull through from the other side with a pair of pliers until the notches have popped into the slot (k).

Screw-top Fittings

On occasion, you may want to use the threaded neck portion of a bottle to attach that bottle to another part of your project. Because the screw top is larger that the neck of the bottle, you can use a Forstner bit to drill a hole just large enough to pass the neck of the bottle through, and then fasten it in place by screwing the cap onto the neck.

Brads and Eyelets

Often used as decorative fasteners, brads and eyelets are now being made in a variety of colors and sizes for scrapbook crafters. They add wonderful details, such as eyes and nostrils, when used as fasteners for your recycled-plastic projects.

Double-Face Foam Adhesive Tape

Some jewelry-related items like pin backs come with a peel-off adhesive strip made from double-face foam adhesive tape. I find that roughing the surface where the pin back will be attached is important. Heating the piece just before applying the adhesive strip, and then compressing the two together with pliers, adds significantly to a successful joint.

Heat Fusing

You can heat plastics to their semi-liquid state to essentially weld them together. This is helpful in some instances, although it is hard to control the soft and sticky plastic when it gets hot enough to fuse. For safety reasons, never heat the plastic to the point of burning.

Forming Techniques

Making and Using Templates

To make a template, transfer one of the patterns provided in the book (or trace a pattern of your own design) onto lightweight cardstock to cut out and use as a template. I find it helpful to hold the template in place on the backside (or wrong side) of the plastic with spring clips in order to trace the outside edge with a fine-point marker (l). Cut along the outside edge of the traced line with sharp scissors (m). It's a good idea to leave extra material on the edges, as you can always trim off the excess but cannot add to the piece once it is cut.

Heat Forming

Once it is cut, most HDPE plastic can be forced into different configurations while it is still cold. You will quickly find, however, that the plastic has a memory and will return to its original molded shape. Gently heat HDPE plastic with a heat gun or a hair dryer to permanently change its shape. Always wear heat-tolerant gloves and be careful not to incinerate plastic, as it can emit toxic fumes (n). After you manipulate the heated plastic, hold it until it cools in its new configuration.

After heating the plastic and before it cools, you can help form its new shape by pressing it against various surfaces, such as a tabletop, a ceramic bowl, or a PVC or metal pipe (o). Once it takes its shape, you can speed up the cooling process by holding it in front of a fan.

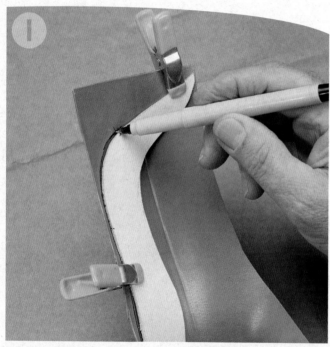

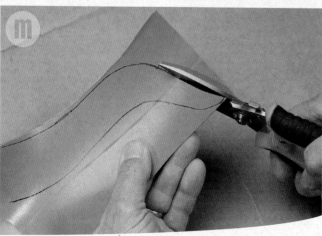

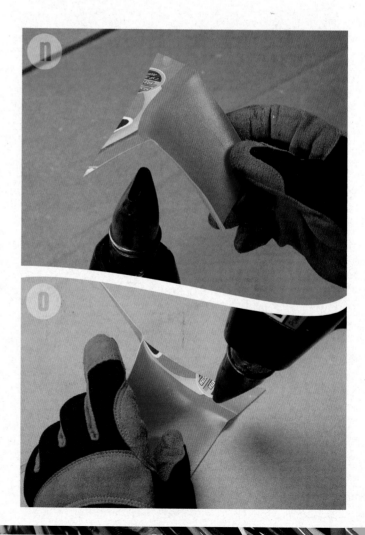

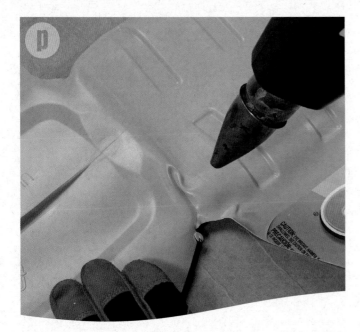

When stretching cut bottles over heat, the material at the ends of cuts will tend to tear. One way to remedy this situation is to punch a ¼-inch (6 mm) or larger hole at the end of each cut, where the material will be stretched (p).

Heat-forming PETE plastic is unpredictable. It is a different type of thermo-forming plastic than HDPE, so it tends to contort uncontrollably. This can be desirable, if that is the effect that you want. In the initial stage of heating, PETE plastic will contract toward the source of heat. Further heating results in a partial liquefaction, causing the plastic to droop. It is unsafe to heat either HDPE or PETE plastic beyond the semi-liquid state.

In some circumstances, I have used heat-forming techniques with PETE plastic. For instance, I will heat the tips of tentacle-like shapes to cause the ends to curl (see the Imaginary Flora project, page 100). I urge you to experiment with this process, as you never know what you can do until you try it.

ROBERT BRADFORD
Toy Soldier, 2007–2008

78¾ x 39⅜ x 39⅜ inches
(200 x 100 x 100 cm)
Recycled plastic toys, wooden
armature; screwed

Photo by artist

Design Considerations

Color

The basic principles of color theory, such as juxtaposition of warm and cool colors for their complementary and contrasting qualities, apply when working with recycled plastic. Fortunately, plastic consumer packaging is already made with focus group-approved colors, so you have many wonderful choices to make your art visually appealing.

Lines

Different kinds of cuts create different lines. Try cutting lines that are both geometric (angular) as well as organic (curved). Most plastic containers are basically organic shapes, so geometric lines result in an unusual and interesting contrast.

Patterns

Try using repetitive cuts or punches to create patterns. I often layer different colors and then punch holes in the top layer to reveal the color of the next layer.

Texture

Most plastic has a very smooth surface, so anything you can do to contrast that adds to the visual interest of your piece. Pinking shears and punches help to create texture. Including parts of the original product label is a fun way to add character. Using frosted translucent plastic from a water jug is another way to add variety.

Layering

Most recyclable plastic comes in a thin, somewhat flat or slightly curved type of shape. Many of the projects in this book involve layering several pieces together, often with the outer layers hiding the fasteners that hold the lower layers in place. Look for ways to layer your compositions for both visual interest and to add to the strength of your constructions.

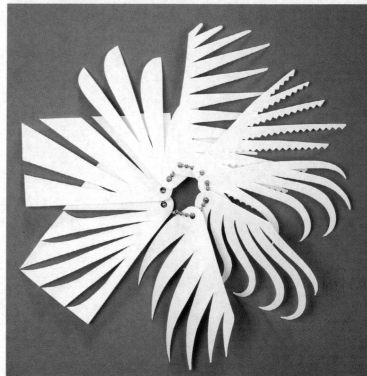

Nesting

Many recyclable plastic parts come in several different sizes, like the different-sized screw caps for different-sized bottles and jars. Nesting smaller components inside larger ones will add more color variety, as it increases the detail.

Shapes

Mixing organic and geometric shapes and using tapered strips is a very effective technique. Symmetrical pieces often lead to successful designs. For wearable pieces, use shapes that are no larger than 2 to 3 inches (5 to 7.6 cm) square and no smaller than a ½-inch (1.3 cm) square of material per piece.

Piscatorial Pins

I created a miniature lapel pin that mimicked my larger sculptures for a museum opening. As I wore it, no one had any trouble identifying which exhibitor I was!

tip: *I like to use the part of the bottle with the label to provide a nice decorative detail.*

This project is a great way to use up smaller scraps of varying hues from other projects. Once you get the hang of how the parts relate to one another, cut loose and create your own designs.

1 Select a fish template from page 137 and cut the armature, leaving a little extra material around the edges. (Unlike a bad haircut, it will not grow if you cut it too short.)

2 Cut out a head and cut a wedge shape for the mouth (page 138), working from the nose-end of the head and ending approximately two-thirds down from the top of the head. Punch a ⅛-inch (3 mm) hole for the eye in between the top of the head and the inside of the mouth.

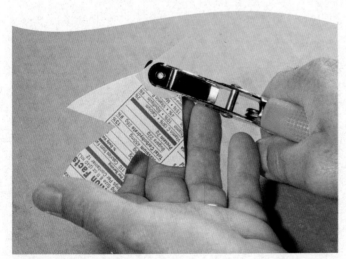

3 Position the head on the armature. Using the eyehole as a guide, punch a hole in the armature that corresponds with the eyehole in the head.

4 Cut a gill shape (page 139) from a third color of plastic, and align it behind the head. Punch a hole that corresponds with the eyehole.

5 Cut a fin from a fourth color of plastic (page 139). Again, use the eyehole in the head as a guide to punch a hole in the fin. Trim the lower edge of the fin with pinking shears to add a decorative effect. Any further detailing of the fin should be done before assembling all of the parts.

6 Punch a hole in a fifth color of plastic for the eye color. This piece needs to be slightly larger than the flange on a pop rivet in order to be seen. Carefully cut a small circle around the outside edge of the hole, creating a doughnut shape similar to a little plastic washer.

7 Stick the blunt end of a small, ⅛-inch (3 mm) pop rivet first through the eye color, then the head, the gill, the pectoral fin, and the body of the fish, in that order. Slip a backing washer over the back end of the assembly, and firmly rivet the pieces together using a compression block.

8 Detail the piece as you desire to define the tail and dorsal and lower fins. If your scissor cuts don't completely release the slivers of plastic, remove the slivers by pulling them toward the backside of the fish to avoid tearing the label.

9 Follow the general gluing instructions on page 30 to add a pinback.

Colorful
Canines

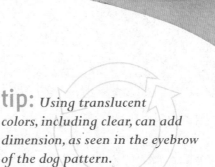

Patterns for the dog on page 126 are just two examples of a canine image. You can develop your own animal design by changing the shape of the silhouette or by replacing the eyebrow with a shape that reflects an eye patch or a droopy ear.

1 Using the templates on page 126 as guides, cut the head, and collar. Punch an eyehole with a ⅛-inch (3 mm) punch. Use a pointed craft knife or crescent-shaped decorative punch to make a shape for the nose.

2 Cut an eyebrow from a different color of plastic, and hold it in alignment with the armature. Make a hole that corresponds with the existing eyehole.

3 Punch a ⅛-inch (3 mm) hole in another color of plastic for the eye color. This piece needs to be slightly larger than the flange on a pop rivet in order to be seen. Cut a small circle around the outside edge of the hole, creating a doughnut shape wide enough to extend beyond the edge of the pop rivet. Thread the blunt end of a pop rivet through the hole in the eye color, into the hole in the eyebrow, and then into the armature. Make sure all three parts will line up the way you want them to look in the finished piece. Disassemble the parts and set them aside.

tip: *Using translucent colors, including clear, can add dimension, as seen in the eyebrow of the dog pattern.*

4 Cut out the collar, making sure that the slot on the collar is wide enough to allow it to lie flat once it is passed over the neck. Slip the collar onto the neck, with the thin part in front and the larger tab behind. Be sure the tab extends behind the eyehole in the head, and make a hole in the tab that aligns with the hole in the armature. Slip the blunt end of the rivet through the holes in the armature and the tab to hold them in their proper places. With a pair of sharp scissors, make a small notch in the armature where the collar sits on the back of the neck.

5 Thread the blunt end of the ⅛-inch (3 mm) pop rivet through the eye color first, then the eyebrow, the armature, and the tab of the collar, in that order. Slip a backing washer over the back end of the assembly, and firmly rivet the pieces together using a compression block.

6 Hot glue a pinback or magnet to the back.

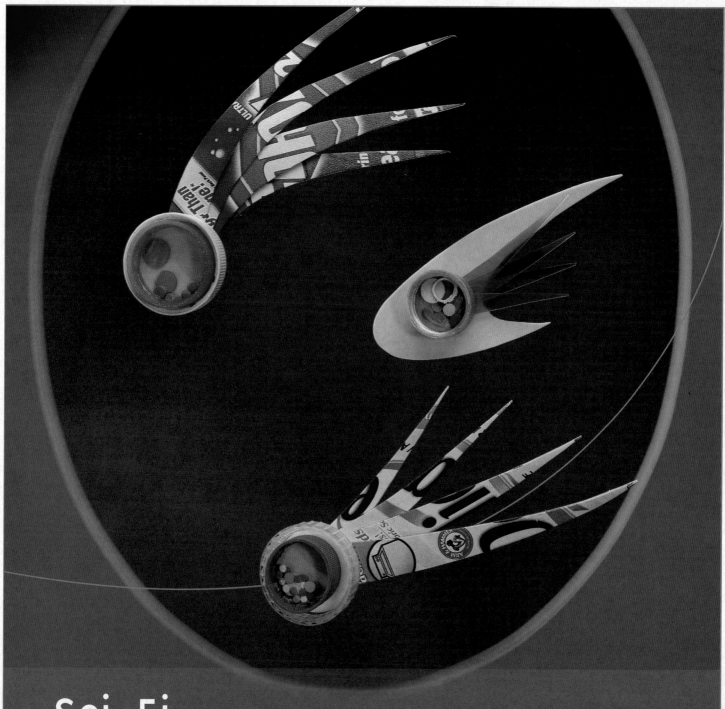

Sci-Fi
Comet

When I work with recycled materials I prefer to leave no scraps behind, so I use the pieces left over to make parts for decorative little projects like the Sci-Fi Comet. Use your imagination to make a variety of fantasy shapes.

1 Select two bottle caps in different colors and sizes; one will need to nest inside the other. Hold them firmly nested together, and drill a 5/32-inch (4 mm) hole through the middle of both caps.

2 Cut a disk from some opaque plastic to line the inside of the smaller cap in order to add background color. . Do not press this part into place yet. That will come later.

3 Cut a second round piece of plastic from the domed section or shoulder of a clear plastic bottle. It should be about the same size as the interior circumference of your smallest bottle cap. You will use this piece in step 6.

4 Cut out four tapered pieces of plastic that have label graphics. They will be used for the comet tail. Arrange the pieces in a fan, overlapping the wider ends. Use masking tape to hold the pieces in place, and drill a 5/32-inch (4 mm) hole where the wide ends of all four pieces overlap.

5 Thread the blunt end of a medium-sized pop rivet through the open end of the nested bottle caps. Add the comet tail onto the pop rivet behind the larger bottle cap, slip a backing washer over the back end of the assembly, and firmly rivet the pieces together, using a compression block.

6 Insert the colored disk inside the smaller cap to cover the pop rivet, and press it into place. Add several tiny scraps of colored plastic that contrast with the background color. Then, fit the clear domed piece into the inner cap, convex side up, to trap the scraps behind the dome.

7 Attach a pinback or magnet to the back.

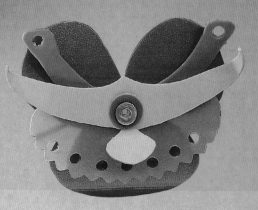

Orchid
Hybrids

The five layers of this project more or less correspond to the scientific descriptions of orchid parts: the dorsal sepal (armature), the petals, the lateral sepals, the callus, and the column. But don't let that scientific jargon scare you: experiment with hole punches, colors of plastic, and make your own shapes for your very own orchid hybrid.

1   Cut the petal section, and use a ⅛-inch (3 mm) punch to make the hole in the center, using the templates on page 127 as guides.

2   Cut the dorsal sepal from translucent plastic. Use pinking shears to cut the jagged edges along the center of the pattern. Punch a matching hole in the center.

3   Cut the lateral sepal, and punch a ⅛-inch (3 mm) hole in the center, as shown. Use ⅛- and 1/16-inch (3 and 1.6 mm) punches to make decorative elements in the center.

4   Cut the callus from another color, and punch a matching hole in the center, as shown.

5   Punch a ⅛-inch (3 mm) hole in another color for the column. Cut a small circle around the outside edge of the hole, creating a doughnut shape wide enough to extend beyond the edge of the pop rivet.

6   Thread the blunt end of the ⅛-inch (3 mm) pop rivet through the column, the callus, the lateral sepal, the dorsal sepal, and the petal, in that order. Slip a backing washer over the back end of the assembly, and firmly rivet the pieces together using a compression block.

7   Attach a pin back or magnet to the back.

Kicky Earrings

My wife, Robin, finds the light weight of recyclable plastics makes kicky costume jewelry. Try some of the following variations or design your own. Now's the perfect time to play with decorative edge scissors and punches.

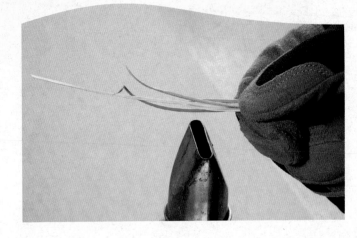

1 Punch ⅟₁₆-inch (4.2 mm) holes in small pieces of plastic to mount them on a head pin. Form an eye at the end of the head pin to attach it to an ear stud, wire, or clip.

3 Heat-fuse the ends of several small, tapered strip-shaped pieces of recyclable plastic. Squeeze the fused end flat with needle-nose pliers while it is still hot. Punch a ⅟₁₆-inch (1.6 mm) hole in the fused end, and trim the end to look finished. Attach the piece to an ear stud, wire, or clip.

2 Punch a ⅟₁₆-inch (4.2 mm) hole in one end of each of several cut and punched plastic shapes to attach the shapes to the eye pin. Add beads, and form an eye at the other end of the pin to attach it to an ear stud, wire, or clip.

Boa
Necklace

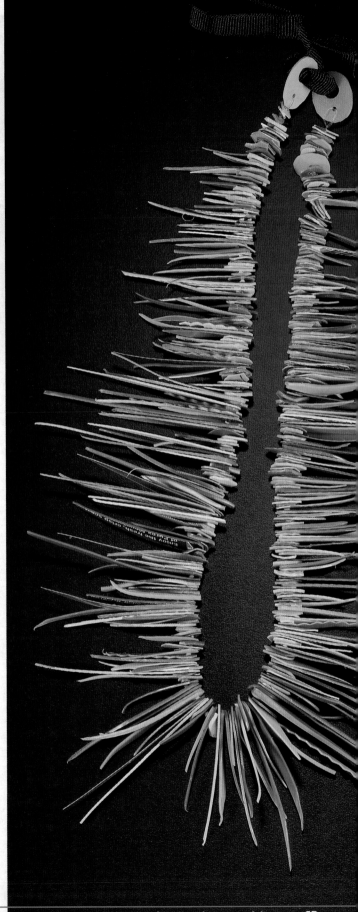

Robin and I were invited to wear our own creative jewelry at an event. Not wanting to disappoint our hosts, Robin asked me to string a necklace with a random assembly of tapered scrap pieces onto a piece of monofilament to match her Kicky Earrings. It was such a hit that I thought I would share the project with you!

1 Punch ¹⁄₁₆-inch (1.6 mm) holes in the wide ends of about 350 to 400 tapered scrap pieces.

2 Trim the ends of the pieces into rough semicircles around the punched holes.

3 String the pieces together to make about 18 inches (45.7 cm) of necklace, using most of the longer pieces toward the center of the string.

4 Punch an additional hole in the final piece on each end in order to tie them together with a piece of ribbon for comfort against the back of the neck.

5 Lay the necklace out on a flat surface, and trim the pieces so it has the finished appearance you desire. It's helpful to blunt sharp ends!

**ELIZABETH GLASS GELTMAN
RACHEL GELTMAN**

Red and Orange Necklace, 2008

24 x 1¼ x ½ inch (61 x 3.2 x 1.3 cm)

Plastic, 14-karat gold wire; pierced, formed, fabricated

Photo by Jeff Geltman

SOFIA CALDERWOOD

White Luster, 2008

11 x 7 x ⅛ inch (27.9 x 17.8 x 0.3 cm)

Plastic produce bags, sterling silver, monofilament; fused, soldered

Photo by artist

GINELLE WEBER

Green with Envy, 2008

22 x 1½ x ½ inch (55.9 x 3.8 x 1.3 cm)

Beach plastic; strung

Photo by Chris Beard

MARGE DILLON
Death to Credit, 2008
1/8 x 2 1/2 inches (0.3 x 6.4 cm)
Copper wire, used credit cards, rivets, plastic children's beads; fabricated, riveted, hand manipulated
Photo by Chris Beard

MINNA KARHU
Picked One Brooch, 2007
4 13/16 x 3 x 2 7/8 inches (12.3 x 7.7 x 7.4 cm)
Recycled plastic, silver, steel; cut, heat shaped, riveted
Photo by artist

CHIA-PEI HSIAO
Propagation V, 2006
11 3/8 x 11 3/8 x 2 3/4 inches (29 x 29 x 7 cm)
Laser cut
Photo by artist

Butterflies Are Free

Who doesn't love butterflies? These fanciful three-dimensional creatures are wonderful on their own or can be used to make fluttering mobiles.

1 Cut the bottom and top rim off of a 1-quart (.95 L) yogurt container. Make a vertical cut down the side of the remaining cylinder opposite the front label. This will result in a fairly flat piece to work with.

2 Fold and crease this piece vertically down the middle of the front label, with the label facing inside.

3 Cut a wing shape from the outer edge of the folded piece, as shown on the templates on page 128, to get a symmetrical pair of connected wings when unfolded. Be sure to reserve the outward-pointing tabs.

4 Using a piece of the scrap from cutting the wings, fold and crease with the label facing out, and cut out the body with legs, head, and antennae (page 128).

5 Cut a ⅜-inch-wide (9.5 mm) rectangular slot along the fold of the body that is ½ inch (1.3 cm) shorter than the length of the fold on the wing piece, with ¼-inch (6 mm) inward-pointing tabs at either end of the slot.

6 Attach the body and wings by gently flexing the body section to fit the wings into the slot, so that the tabs overlap the ends of the crease in the wing section. Reinforce with glue, if desired.

Uncommon
Insects

T hese six-legged creatures are easy and fun to make, especially for kids to use as tricks on unsuspecting friends and siblings.

BUG

1 I like to use quart-size (.95 L) yogurt tubs for this project—the lightweight material is easy to cut and fold by hand. Use the basic design, following the template on page 129 as a guide for your bug, and then let your creative instincts conjure up your own creepy-crawly variations.

2 Fold a curved piece of plastic perpendicular to the curve to establish a centerline reference. You can also use a dry-erase marker to mark the centerline.

3 Cut out the mouth area and outside curves of the antennae, starting at the front of your bug.

4 Cut out the inside curves of the antennae and legs, working from front to back, as shown. Alternating sides as you cut out each leg helps to keep your piece balanced.

5 Use a ⅟₁₆- or ⅛-inch (1.6 or 3 mm) punch to make the eyeholes, as shown.

6 Fold antennae upward, and fold eyes, mouth, and legs downward for the desired bug-like effect.

GRASSHOPPER/CRICKET

This piece, a variation of the Bug, is made with a coffee can lid. You'll swear it will chirp once it's done. Use the template on page 130, and then follow the instructions for the Bug, except fold the rear set of legs up instead of down.

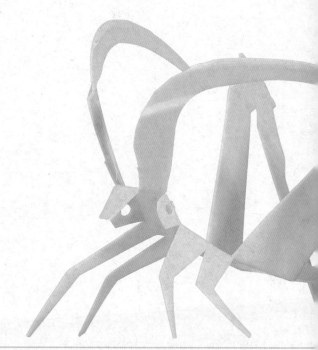

Artie the Arachnid

One simple spider makes a Halloween decoration, but imagine the screams an entire nest of them would create.

1 I find that the thick bottom panel of a bottle works best for the spider. The heavier plastic helps it stand up, and you can use the mold seam as a centerline reference.

2 Cut the piece according to the template on page 131, and then heat-form to fold the legs down and out for the best effect.

3 Heat-form to tilt the abdomen up at the hip while rolling the outside edges under.

4 Heat-form to shape the head by folding the mouth area down, followed by wrapping the eyes toward the front.

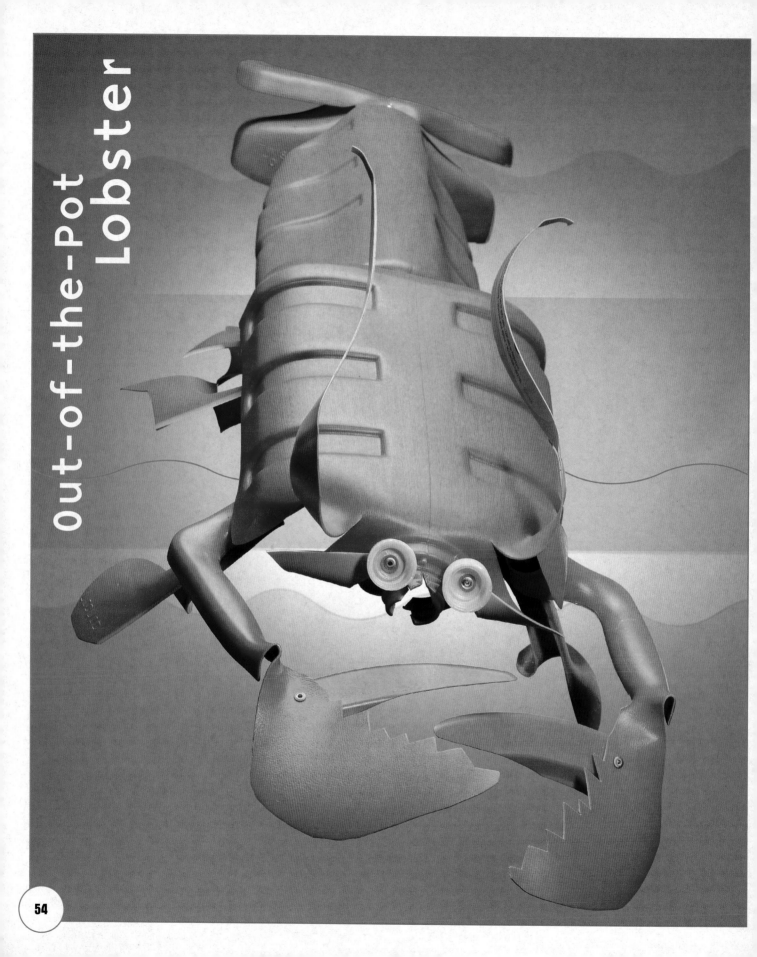

Out-of-the-Pot Lobster

Although not as tasty with drawn butter as the real thing, this feisty bottom-feeding crustacean makes a great wall display. You will need two 300-ounce (8.9L) square bottles with handles and three large jugs to bring this red creature to life.

1 Cut a squarish bottle with a handle into thirds, vertically, starting at both ends of the handle and going down and all the way around both sides. The section with the larger spout opening will become the main body or carapace. The section with the smaller opening will become the tail. The middle section, with most of the labels and the handle, is just scrap.

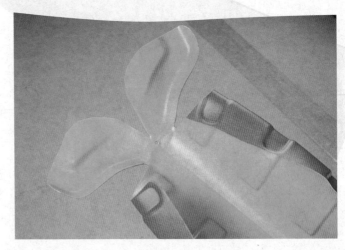

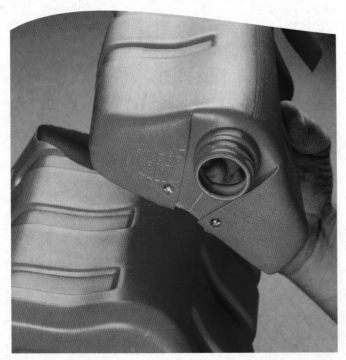

2 Cut, gather, and rivet the end around the smaller opening (the tail section) to narrow the width. This end will attach to the carapace.

3 Cut and heat-form the fin end of the tail section, as shown, to make the first two fins of the tail.

4 Heat-form a taper in the tail section, rolling and tucking in the sides at the end with the fins.

5 Cut additional tail fins, and attach with pop rivets.

6 Drill a hole in the bottom panel of the carapace section with a Forstner drill bit. The hole should be the size of the spout on the tail section.

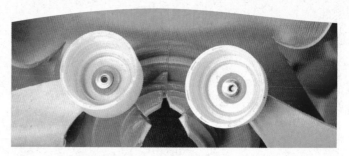

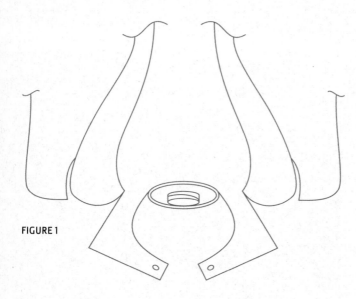

FIGURE 1

7 Cut the carapace section for antennae and eye stalks, as shown in the illustration (figure 1), and drill holes for attaching the eyepieces to the eyestalks.

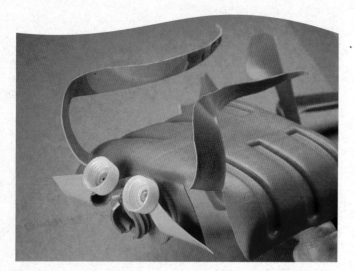

8 Heat-form the antennae and eyestalks. Use a spring clip to hold the antennae together for symmetrical composition.

9 Attach small screw-cap eyes to the eyestalks, and make symmetrical mouth and head details from the remaining spout material.

10 Divide all three handle sections along the mold seam lines to make sets of legs. Be sure to keep the transom and shoulder material attached.

11 Arrange leg sets symmetrically, and staple the transom sections together.

12 Cut the top fourth of your second suitcase bottle for the claws. Remove the cuff section behind the handle, and divide the remaining handle and end material along the mold-seam lines to make matching right and left claws.

13 Shape and heat-form the larger backhand section of each claw with a sawtooth edge.

14 Cut thumbs from the curb section of the bottle, and attach them to the claws with pop rivets.

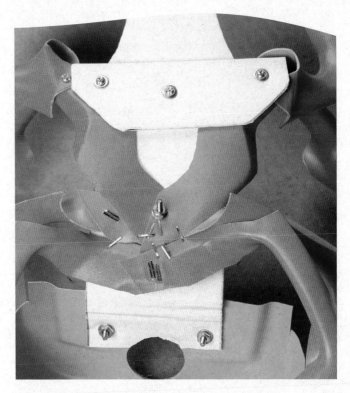

15 Cut a large, sturdy piece of scrap to make a mounting strip for the legs. Fit the strip to the rear of the carapace with a hinge tab.

16 Attach the leg assembly and claws to the mounting strip using staples, and attach a hanger wire to the outside of the mounting strip using a pop rivet or a machine screw. This can be messy, so improvise!

17 Trim the remaining shoulder ends of the legs for feet, and cut the end of the mounting strip to fit snugly behind the head and mouth.

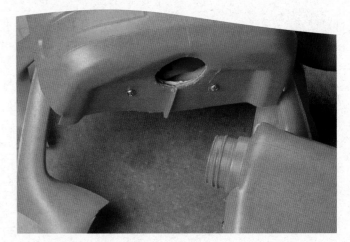

18 Attach the tail section to the carapace by pushing the small spout of the tail section through the hole made in the carapace, and screw an appropriate-sized cap onto the spout to hold it in place.

Crustaceans

I get a bit crabby when I don't get to work in my studio. If I simply feel the need to make something I often make a crustacean or two. They're permanent denizens of my Plastiquarium environments and only have three components: legs, head, and body.

SMALL CRAB (TWO-PIECE)

1 Cut the legs and claws from the bottom two-thirds of a quart-size yogurt container or margarine tub.

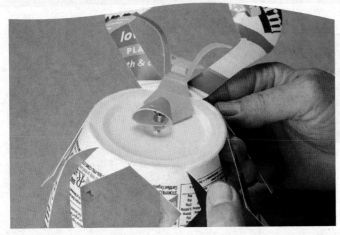

2 Cut the head from a different color, and punch ⅛-inch (3 mm) holes for the eyes. Cut a large tab from another scrap piece, and attach with a pop rivet, first going through the head (or neck) and then the legs.

3 Make the shell from a lid of a large bottle, cutting one edge away for the head to emerge. A hacksaw works well for cutting thicker, rigid materials for this piece.

4 Glue the shell to the scrap tab connected to the head.

LARGE CRAB (TWO-PIECE)

1 Cut the legs and claws along with the head with attached antennae all in one piece, using the bottom and edges of a standard-size HDPE detergent bottle. Note: Use a small heat gun as you twist and fold these extremities with needle-nose pliers.

2 Make the shell from any convex bottle panel that is symmetrical and big enough.

3 Attach the two sections together with a pop rivet, and add a 6-inch (15.2 cm) piece of copper wire on the bottom to hang your crab on the wall.

3-D Fish

Have you made large schools of colorful flat fish brooches? Now it's time to move on to other dimensions and bring them to life in 3-D. These tropical creatures were inspired by the bright colors and plentiful marine life of my home state of Florida.

1 Select a large, tapered, flat bottle for the body, such as a PETE squeezable bottle that dishwashing liquid comes in. Remove the labels.

2 Cut the head, jaw, and gill pieces from several colors of HDPE plastic. Note: You will need to determine how they will fit onto the body, as shown. Tape these pieces in place and drill holes for pop rivets.

3 Cut out the pectoral fins. Drill holes, and attach the pectoral fins with pop rivets along the sides of the bottom end of the body.

4 Attach the head, jaw, and gills with pop rivets. Be sure the gills cover the pop rivets on the pectoral fins. Note: Use an extension magnet to position steel backing washers inside the jug. Pop the rivets onto the backing washers.

5 Select various sizes of bottle caps for the eyes, and nest them together. Attach the eyes to the head with machine screws.

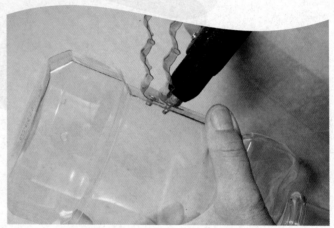

6 Cut the abdominal and dorsal fins, and attach them to the body with pop rivets.

7 Fill the body with colorful scraps of HDPE.

8 Make the tail from the top of a small HDPE bottle, and attach its cap to the cap of the body's bottle with a machine screw. Screw the caps onto their bottles, as shown.

Slithery
Serpent

Reptiles, especially serpents, have always fascinated me. (Much to my mother's dismay, I once came home from school with a five-foot yellow rat snake wrapped around my arms.) Since snakes are so flexible, making them from recycled plastic works like a charm (pun intended!).

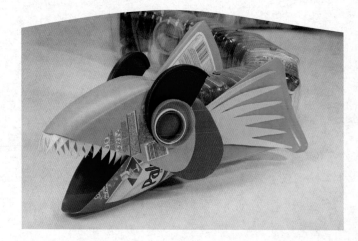

1 Cut tabs, as shown (figure 1), on at least six matching PETE bottles (leave a seventh similar PETE bottle with a screw top uncut to attach to the tail). Punch a ⅛-inch (3 mm) hole in the center of each tab in order to connect them with pop rivets to form the body.

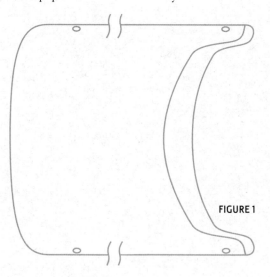

FIGURE 1

2 Cut the head, jaw, and gill pieces from several colors of HDPE plastic. You will need to determine how these pieces will fit onto the bottom part of the first PETE bottle, as shown. Cut the teeth from a separate piece of white HDPE plastic to insert in the head, as shown (optional). Tape these pieces in place, and drill holes for pop rivets.

3 Cut out fins (optional). Drill holes, and attach them with pop rivets along the sides of the bottom end of the first bottle.

4 Attach the jaw, gills, and head with teeth (if you included teeth) to each other. Note: Be sure the gills cover the pop rivets on the fins (if you made fins). (This is similar to making the head for the 3-D Fish on page 60).

5 Select various sizes of bottle caps for the eyes. Nest them

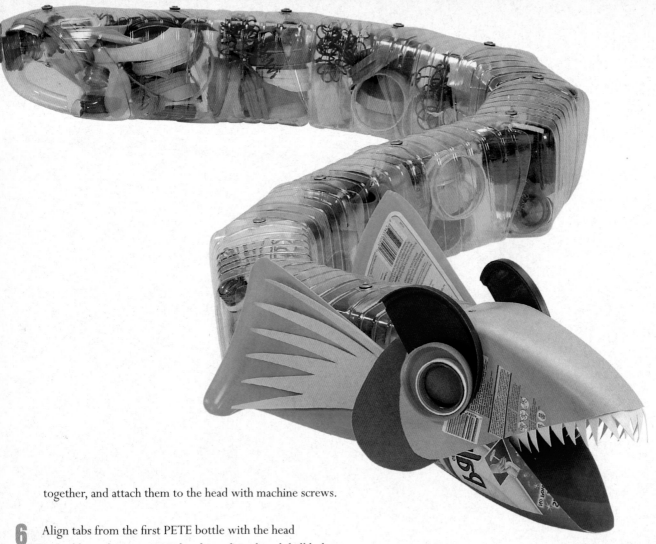

together, and attach them to the head with machine screws.

6 Align tabs from the first PETE bottle with the head assembly to the next PETE bottle, and mark and drill holes for pop rivets.

7 Fill the first bottle with chunky scraps of HDPE. Make sure the pieces are large enough so they do not fall out of small openings.

8 Pop rivet these two PETE bottles together. Reduce stress on these connections with loosely placed washers on both ends of the pop rivets.

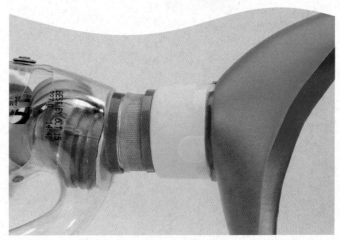

9 Repeat steps 6, 7, and 8 for the remaining PETE bottles.

10 Add the uncut PETE bottle to the end of the serpent. Use an extension magnet to position steel backing washers for the rivets.

11 Make the tail from the top of a small HDPE bottle, and

attach its cap to the cap of the end bottle with a machine screw. Screw the caps onto their bottles, as shown.

Birds in Flight

This soaring bird in flight is made from the handle side of almost any jug bottle. It's a little tricky to make at first, but so is taking that first flight from the nest. A flock of these birds makes a great mobile (see page 112).

1 Using the template on page 132 as a guide, cut the bottom panel and the neck from a standard-handled jug bottle, leaving as much shoulder material as possible.

2 Cut from the outside corners of the bottom edge of the transom up to the outside edges of the handle, where it connects to the transom, and then cut around the inside bottom of the handle, separating the cuff from the bottom of the handle. Note: These cuts result in the tail section of your bird.

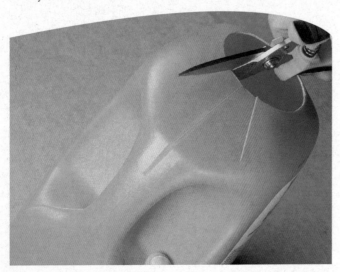

3 Make cuts, starting ½ inch (1.3 cm) from either side of the mold seam above the handle, radiating down from the neck to just above the bottom of the shoulder. Note: This roughs in the head area.

4 Turn the cuts made in step 3 outward, and continue cutting around the outside edges of the cuff until the cuts reach the starting point made in step 2. Note: At this point, your piece should separate from the rest of the bottle and begin to take shape.

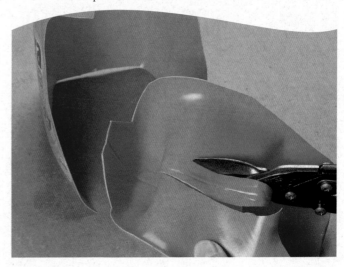

5 Separate the wings of your bird at the middle of the bottom of the cuff by making a pair of curved cuts that meet at the top of the cuff behind the top of the handle. This will remove an elongated wedge that includes the cuff section of the mold seam.

6 Refine the inner and outer edges of the wings as necessary. Extend the curvature of the shoulder area of the wings by cutting about 1 inch (2.5 cm) farther along the cuff edge behind the bird's neck.

7 Heat-form to spread the wings, tucking the wing shoulders behind the bird's neck at the location of the cuts in step 6.

8 Refine the shape of the tail section, and make cuts for an odd number of feathers.

9 Make feather cuts, starting at the outside ends of the wings. Alternate each feather cut between wings to create a balanced appearance. Note: Use a slight wedge shape for feather cuts.

10 Cut the shape of the head, neck, and beak, as shown. Heat-form the sides of the head up, and angle the neck and beak down. Drill or punch ⅛-inch (3 mm) holes for the eyes.

11 Find the balance point to display your bird on a length of monofilament or a mobile (page 112).

Not-So-Dreadful Dragon

One morning, excited about a project I was working on, I rolled out of bed and right into the studio without even brushing my teeth. My wife came out to kiss me good morning and complained that I had dragon breath. In spite of that, she really loves this variation of the dreaded serpent with horns, wings, legs, and spikes.

Tip: *Bulk snack foods are often sold in large PETE jars.*

1 Select two large multi-gallon PETE jars for the body. Arrange them so the openings face each other. One of the openings will need to fit inside the other. You may need to enlarge one of the openings to achieve this.

2 Drill two holes about 1 inch (2.5 cm) apart on either side of the center of the bottoms of each jar. Connect them together as indicated in step 1, using a loop of strong elastic similar to bungee cord material. Do not tie the elastic so tightly that you cannot untie it.

3 Select two matching pairs of large-handled HDPE bottles to make the legs. Cut out the handles, keeping all neck, shoulder, and transom material attached. Note: Do not cut off the extra material around the transom; retain all of the area's curb and side panel edges.

4 Heat-form at the middle of each handle, twisting and bending at a right angle to make the dog-leg angle for the leg pieces, as shown. To achieve symmetrical pairs for the right and left sides, alternate the direction you twist and bend the leg for each side.

5 Cut the shoulder areas of each leg piece to make claw feet.

6 Position and cut the transom section of the legs to fit against the front and rear sections of the PETE body.

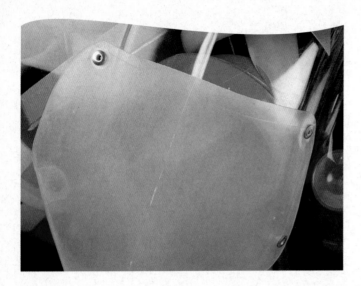

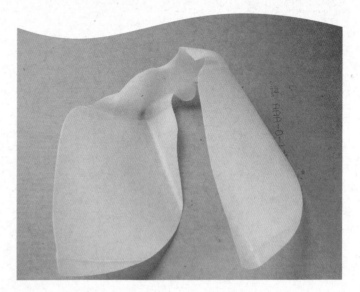

7 Drill holes to attach the legs to the PETE body sections with pop rivets. You will need to disconnect the elastic to do this.

8 Select the appropriately sized PETE bottles or jars to serve as the neck and base of the tail. Drill two holes in the bottom of each bottle that match the holes in the body in order for the elastic to connect all the way through.

9 Cut away the open end of the container for the tail base. Be sure to leave the upper and lower tabs about 1 inch (2.5 cm) long and about 1½ inches (3.8 cm) wide to attach additional segments of the tab. (See the serpent illustration on page 63.)

10 Select additional PETE containers to complete the tail. Cut away the ends as directed in step 9, except the one for the tip of the tail, which you leave uncut. Note: Each container should be smaller than the previous one to affect the overall tapered shape of the tail.

11 Punch ⅛-inch (3 mm) holes in the center of each tab, and drill corresponding holes in the bottoms of the next bottles to prepare them to be pop riveted together in the same manner as the segments for the serpent (see page 62–63).

12 Cut out a pair of connected wings for your dragon (without wings, it will look more like a dinosaur).

Tip: *Large kitty-litter containers work well for wings.*

13 Use bottle-handle sections for spikes. Cut them at an angle; punch holes to attach them.

14 Drill or punch holes in the wings to attach them with pop rivets to the shoulder area of the torso. Attach a row of back spikes in the same manner.

15 Cut the head from the end and side panels of an HDPE bottle that has an elongated shape, keeping as much of the end panel side of the shoulder as possible.

16 Cut out a jaw piece and teeth from another HDPE bottle that fits with the head.

17 Select a PETE container, and cut tabs in it to attach it to the neck. Assemble the head in a manner similar to assembling the head of the serpent (see page 63), attaching it to the tabbed PETE container. You will attach this to the neck piece later, using pop rivets.

18 Design eyes made from assorted screw caps, and cut shapes for the horns from the curb section of an HDPE bottle. Attach the eyes and horns to the head.

19 Assemble the dragon using the elastic, and filling the head, torso, and hip sections with plastic scrap or any colorful material of your choice. Permanently tie the elastic inside the base of the tail section.

20 Assemble the tail segments, enclosing material inside each section.

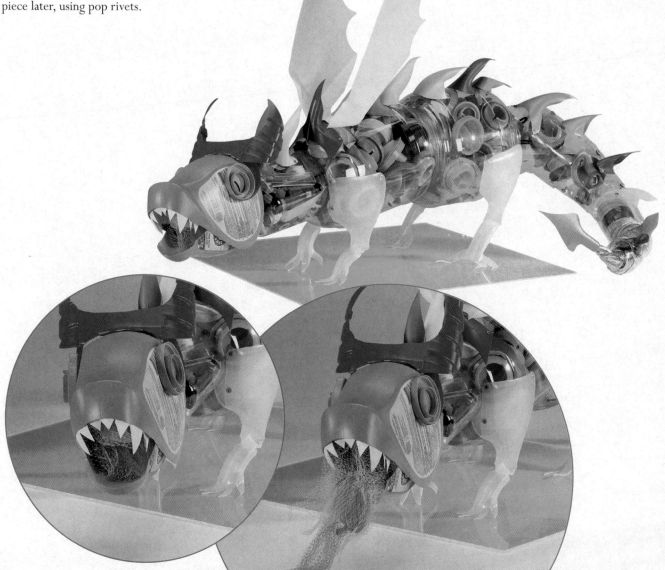

Gallery

LANA SHUTTLEWORTH

Where Will They Go?, 2007

48 x 96 x 3 inches (121.9 x 243.8 x 7.6 cm)

Safety cones, recycled stage flooring; hand carved, nailed

Photo by Kelly Fajack

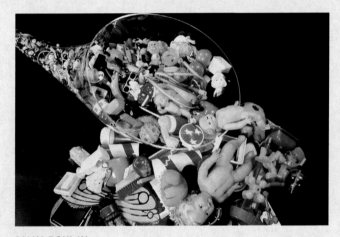

DIANA BOULAY

Witness, 1985

21¼ x 36³/₁₆ x 100³/₈ inches (54 x 92 x 255 cm)

Plastic found objects, acrylic; strewn

Photo by Daniel Roussel

EDWARD LANE MCCARTNEY

Plastolier, 2008

36 x 13 x 13 inches (91.4 x 33 x 33 cm)

Recycled plastic water bottle, steel; heat formed

Photo by artist

YUKA SAITO

Sea Flower (Brooch), 2005

3¹⁵⁄₁₆ x 3¹⁄₈ x 1¹⁵⁄₁₆ inches (10 x 8 x 5 cm)

Recycled polypropylene, nylon, sterling silver; heat shaped, hand formed

Photo by artist

JOHN DAHLSEN

Primary Totems, 2000

86⁵⁄₈ x 19¹¹⁄₁₆ x 19¹¹⁄₁₆ inches (220 x 50 x 50 cm)

Australian beach plastic, 316 stainless steel, steel

Photo by Mark Gerritsen

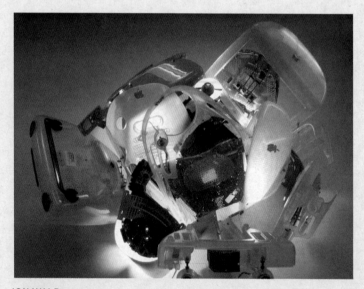

JON WALD

Crash Bootcamp, 2008

50 x 54 x 16 inches (127 x 137.2 x 40.6 cm)

Recycled computers, sockets, bulbs; bolted

Photo by artist

The Dove

Holiday decorations are a great way to create unique family collectibles. I learned how to make this dove from my former art teacher, Lucien Lavoie. It's so simple: all you need is an empty bleach bottle and a good pair of scissors. Hang one on a tree or make a mobile!

1 Cut the threaded portion of the neck off of the bottle, and cut the web that connects the upper end of the handle to the neck of the bottle, taking care not to damage the upper end of the handle.

2 Cut around the curves of the outer edges of the cuff on both sides of the handle, stopping about 1 inch (2.5 cm) short of the mold seam at the bottom of the handle.

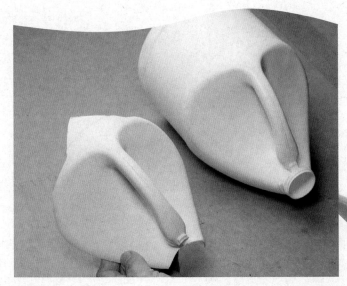

3 Continue the cuts at a downward angle so that they join at the mold seam about 2 inches (5 cm) below the end of the handle, creating a triangular shape at the bottom of the handle. This separates the work piece from the remainder of the bottle.

4 Separate the wings of your bird at the middle on the top of the cuff by making a pair of curved cuts that meet at the bottom of the cuff behind the bottom of the handle. This will remove an elongated wedge that includes the cuff section of the mold seam.

5 Cut the head and neck from the triangle created in step 3, making sure the point of the triangle lines up with the beak of the bird. Punch ⅛-inch (3 mm) holes for the eyes, and make a symmetrical crease along the centerline of the head, neck, and beak by folding and squeezing with pliers. Refine all of the cut edges with trimming scissors.

6 Find the balance point of the dove, and attach a piece of lightweight wire for display.

Festive
Garland

You'll find that you generate a great deal of scrap making the projects in this book. In my studio I have bins of the long, slender tapers from refining the outside edges of larger pieces or detailing fins of fish. This project is another way to recycle by transforming these castoff, colorful bits into festive garlands.

1 Punch a ¹⁄₁₆-inch (1.6 mm) hole in each piece you intend to use. String pieces onto a 15- to 20-pound (6.8 to 9 kg) monofilament thread. Experiment with orienting the curve of each piece as you work to create your own decorative effects.

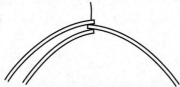

2 Use spacers, or beads like the caps in the Holiday Wreath project on page 80, to extend the length of your work.

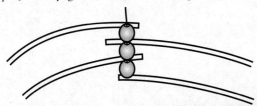

3 Twenty or more plastic scraps are needed to achieve a single inch (2.5 cm) of finished garland when they're strung flat side to flat side. Another way to stretch out designs is to punch two holes in each piece and run the thread through both of them.

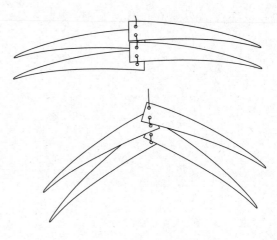

4 Use the locking tab and slot connection, as shown, to link plastic scraps together into a chain as an alternate to threading your work.

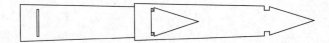

snowflakes

After making a flock of doves, I was left with a lot of white scrap, so I made wintry holiday decorations. The snowflake project is about as simple as they come and is also the basic component of the wreath project (page 80). And who says you can't have blue snowflakes if you wish?

1 Cut four strips of white plastic, about ½ to 1 inch (1.3 to 2.5 cm) wide and about 8 inches (20.3 cm) long, from around the barrel section of a bleach bottle.

2 Punch a ⅛-inch (3 mm) hole near the center of each strip, and trim the ends of each strip to a taper. Note: You can also detail the ends of the strips with pinking shears and various-shaped punches for a more decorative effect.

3 Cut a piece of monofilament, about 10 inches (25.4 cm) long, and tie a small loop in each end to serve as a hanger.

4 Assemble your piece on a pop rivet with one of the loops sandwiched in the middle.

5 Alternate the orientation of the curve of each of the four plastic strips to give the piece good dimension.

6 Arrange the strips, and pop the rivet using a backing washer and a compression block.

Holiday
Wreath

$\mathbf{T}$his classic holiday decoration will really stand up to the weather. I used about two years' worth of screw caps from half-and-half cartons (yes, that's approximately 100) and about 6 feet (1.8 m) of white 12-gauge insulated copper wire. For a more natural look, use green plastic scraps!

1 Cut the scrap bottles into roughly ½- to 1-inch-wide (1.3 to 2.5 cm) strips, about 6 to 9 inches (15.2 to 22.9 cm) long, tapering at one or both ends. These strips do not need to be uniform, so you can use most of the bottle except the flat bottom panel. Curves are good, so plan your cutting to result in curved pieces.

2 Punch ⅛-inch (3 mm) holes near the center of each plastic strip.

3 Drill ⅛-inch (3 mm) holes in the center of each screw cap.

4 Twist a tight loop in one end of the wire, and start stringing with a screw cap so the open end covers the loop.

5 String sets of four plastic strips (like the Snowflakes on page 78) with one screw cap between each set. Alternate the curvature of each strip as you add it, and also alternate the direction of each cap added between sets.

6 Fasten the ends of the wire together tightly when you have strung enough strip sets and caps to complete your wreath circle.

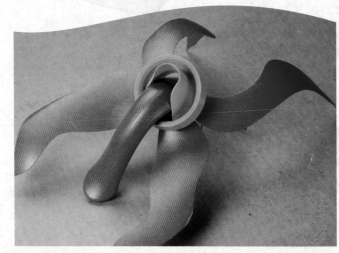

7 Make a flower or bow accent from colored plastic, as shown.

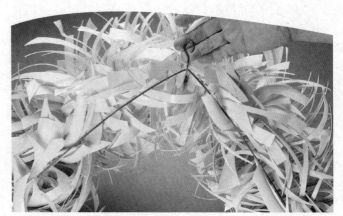

8 Make a support frame from stiff wire for the back of the wreath. This will function as a hanger and help keep the shape of your wreath.

Gallery

**ANAT DAHARI
YONATAN MATSREE
ADAM GIBSON**

Geodesic Dome, 2005

90⁹/₁₆ x 55⅛ inches (230 x 140 cm)

Plastic bottles; heat formed

Photos by Avi Sonego

KIM CONOVER-LOAR

Orangeyougladtoseeme?, 2007

10 x 7 x 15 inches (25.4 x 17.8 x 38.1 cm)

Recycled plastic; cut, riveted, heat bent

Photo by Steve Loar 0223d

HEATH NASH

Lillyball, 2007

15¾ inches (40 cm) in diameter

Yogurt bottles, soda lids, wire; cut, creased

Photo by Dave Southwood

MICHELLE SALES

Bound One, 2007

10 x 12 x 10 inches (25.4 x 30.5 x 25.4 cm)

Recycled synthetic packing felts, curly willow branched, encaustic paints, silicone glue; heat treated, shaped, hand sewn

Photo by Jonathan Sales

DODI REIFENBERG

Jackie O, 2007

33⁷/₈ x 26³/₄ inches (86 x 68 cm)

Plastic bags, cellophane tape

Photo by Trevor Morgan

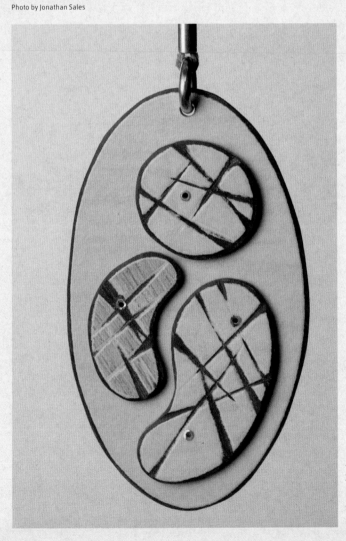

LEIGH WAGNER

Sawn Timber, 2008

2³/₄ x 1⁹/₁₆ x ³/₁₆ inch (7 x 4 x 0.5 cm)

Recycled kitchen laminate, sterling silver; hand sewn, filed, riveted

Photo by Anna Jacobson

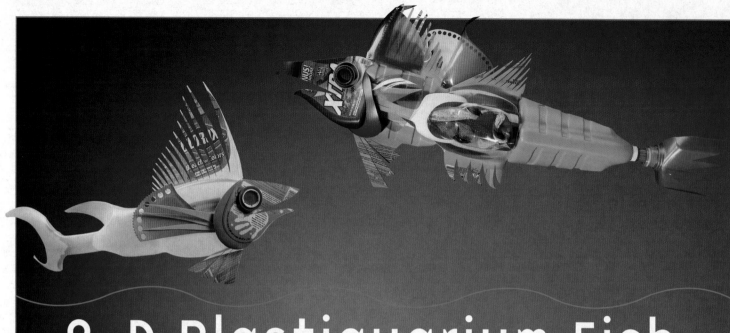

2-D Plastiquarium Fish

I've created a fantasy marine ecosystem called the Plastiquarium filled with fishlike creatures that use the packaging that can pollute our environment. Once you choose one of the body types for the armature, you can embellish it to your heart's content.

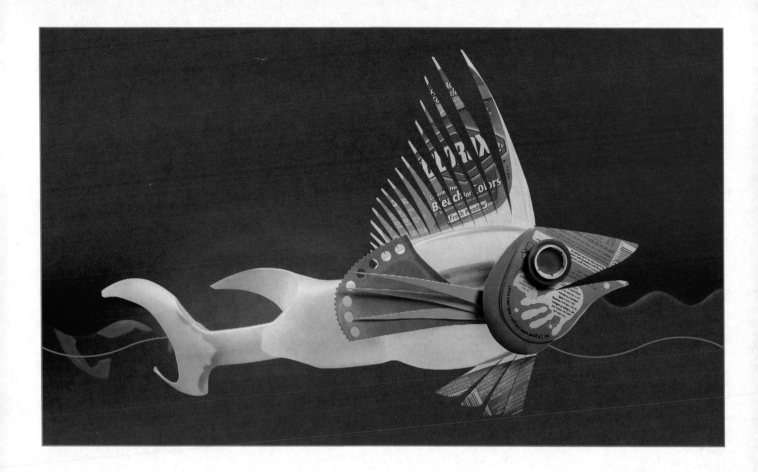

HANDLETAIL

1 Using the template on page 133 as a guide for cutting, remove the spout and cut from the top of the mold seam of the end panel to the bottom edge of the shoulder.

3 Cut down from the slice at the shoulder along the edges of all four panels to the curb at the bottom of the bottle. Tip: End each of these cuts with a ¼-inch (6 mm) or larger hole.

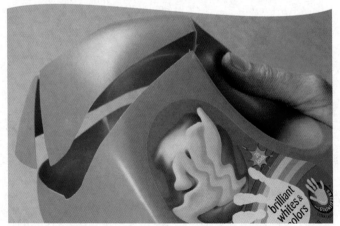

2 Cut a T at the end of the previous slice and cut around the shoulder edge, passing through the top of the cuff behind the handle.

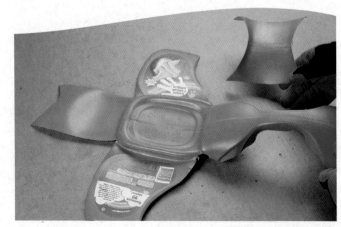

4 Heat-form and fold open all four panels along the curb, forming a generally flat shape with the bottom panel at the center.

5 Cut away the cuff material behind the handle.

6 Cut a V-shape out of the top of the inside of the handle where the handle curves the most.

7 Heat-form, stretch, and flex the curved section of the handle so the shoulder and handle align with the transom.

8 Hold the shoulder section against a flat, heat-tolerant surface. Spread out the tail fins, and use heat to relax the shape. Massage the shape of the fins with a gloved hand as they cool.

9 Cut away any excess perimeter material, and refine the shape of the tail fins as desired.

SWALLOWTAIL

1 Using the template on page 133 as a cutting guide, remove the spout, and cut down the mold seam on the handle side well into the top of the handle (about 4 inches [10.2 cm]). Then cut down the mold seam of the end panel, about halfway to the bottom of the bottle.

2 Cut a T at the end of your cut into the top of the handle, and continue cutting just below the edge of the shoulder on both sides. Then turn these cuts down the outside edges of the end panel to the curb at the bottom of the bottle. End each of these cuts with a ¼-inch (6 mm) or larger hole.

3 Cut down the edges of the handle panel to the curb at the bottom of the bottle, and make ¼-inch (6 mm) or larger holes at the ends.

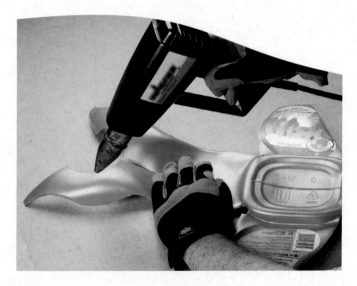

4 Heat-form and fold open all four panels along the curb, forming a generally flat shape with the bottom panel at the center.

5 Cut away the handle and cuff section above the transom.

6 Hold the shoulder section against a flat, heat-tolerant surface to begin to spread out the tail area. Use heat to relax the shape.

7 Cut out a wavy, tapered shape from one side of the tail section, as shown in the photo above/below/at right.

8 Trace and cut out a cardboard pattern from the shape made in the previous step.

9 Flip over your pattern to trace and cut out a matching shape for the other side of the swallowtail. Note: I like to use small spring clips to hold cardboard against plastic for tracing.

10 Hold the tail section against a flat, heat-tolerant surface to finish spreading out the tail area. Use heat to relax the plastic. Massage the shape of the tail fins with a gloved hand as they cool and set.

11 Cut away any excess perimeter material, and refine the shapes as desired.

RUFFLETAIL

1 Using the template on page 134 as a cutting guide, remove the spout, and cut down the mold seam on the handle side well into the top of the handle (about 2 to 3 inches [5 to 7.6 cm]).

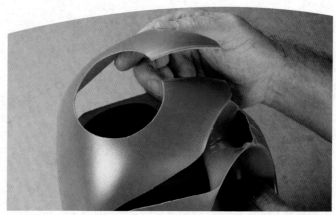

2 Cut a T at the end of your cut into the top of the handle, and continue cutting just below the edge of the shoulder on both sides. Then turn these cuts down the outside edges of the end panel to the curb at the bottom of the bottle. End each of these cuts with a ¼-inch (6 mm) or larger hole.

3 Cut down the edges of the handle panel to the curb at the bottom of the bottle, and make ¼-inch (6 mm) or larger holes at the ends.

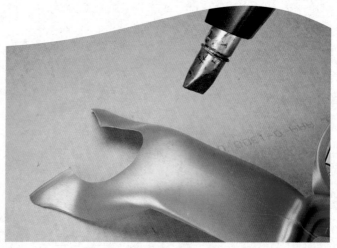

4 Heat-form and fold open all four panels along the curb, forming a generally flat shape with the bottom panel at the center.

5 Cut away the handle and cuff section above the transom.

6 Hold the shoulder section against a flat, heat-tolerant surface to begin to spread out the tail area. Use heat to relax the shape.

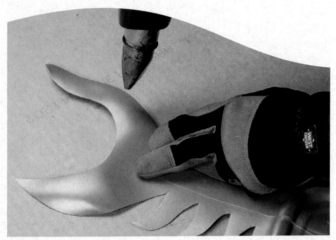

7 Determine the top edge, based on the direction you want your fish to swim, and trim away about half of the material above the mold seam between the shoulder and the curb, as shown.

8 Carefully cut out a row of tapered slivers along the bottom edge of the tail, starting with the leading edge of the bottom tail fin.

9 Trim the main tail fins, and hold the tail section against a flat, heat-tolerant surface to finish spreading out the tail area. Use heat to relax the plastic. Massage the shape of the tail fins with a gloved hand as they cool and set.

10 Cut away any excess perimeter material, and refine the shapes as desired.

SUITCASE

Use a 300-ounce (8.9 L) "suitcase" bottle with the handle on top and a spigot for this fish.

1 Using the template on page 135 as a cutting guide, cut across the top panel, starting just inside the smaller plain screw cap (vent), with neck and threads intact and attached. Continue cutting down the edges of the vent end panel down to the curb. End each of these cuts with a ¼-inch (6 mm) or larger hole.

2 Determine locations for cuts by envisioning the bottle unfolding with the vent end panel as the tail extension, the bottom panel as the abdomen, and the spigot end panel as the chest. Leave the front and back label panels attached to where you want fins on the chest and abdomen area.

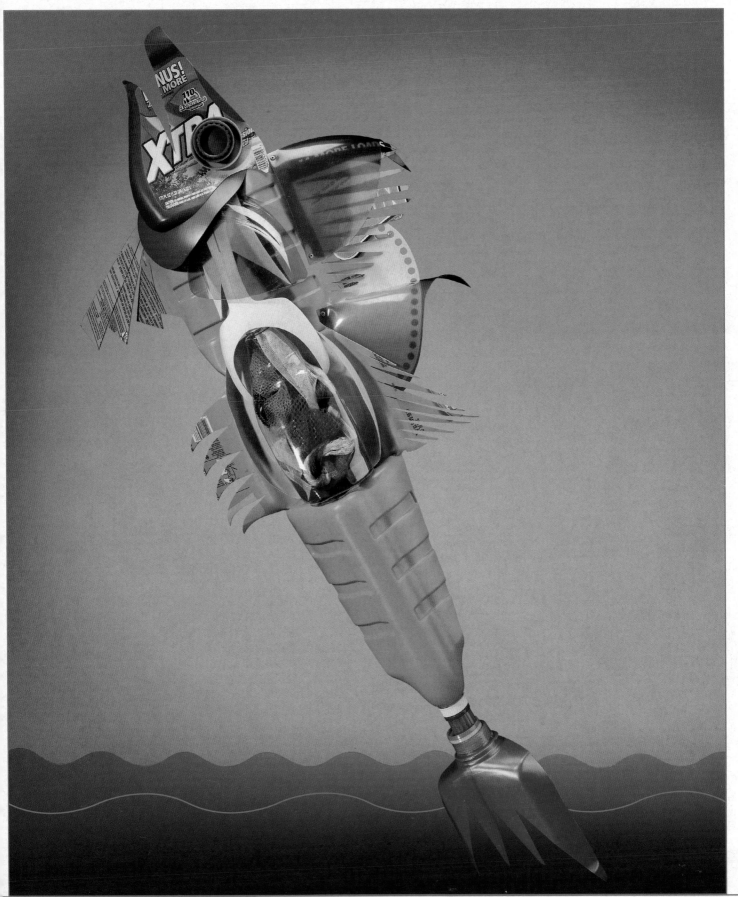

3 Cut and heat-form to fold open the bottle as described in step 2.

4 Taper the vent panel toward the threaded vent neck to establish the appearance of the tail section.

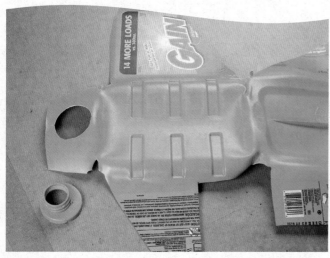

5 Remove the threaded spigot neck and handle. Make cuts to that area, and heat-form to fold open the remaining material. This extension becomes the tab where you attach the head.

6 Cut away any excess perimeter material, and refine the shapes as desired.

7 Cut a tail from the top of a flattish squeeze-type bottle, keeping the threaded neck and cap intact. Dish detergent bottles are good for this.

8 Drill holes in both the vent and the tail cap, and attach the two caps back to back with a machine screw. Then, use the connected screw caps as a coupling to join the two parts together.

PIGGY BANK

Use a 150-ounce (4.5 L) "piggy bank" bottle with a spigot for this fish.

1 Using the template on page 135 as a guide, cut across the top panel, starting just inside the smaller plain screw cap (vent), with the neck and threads intact and attached. Continue cutting around the connection of the handle to the cuff, separating the vent end of the handle from the shoulder area of the bottle.

2 Cut along the mold seam in the cuff behind the handle, and fork the cut at the bottom of the cuff to continue down both sides of the transom to the curb at the bottom of the bottle. End each of these cuts with a ¼-inch (6 mm) or larger hole.

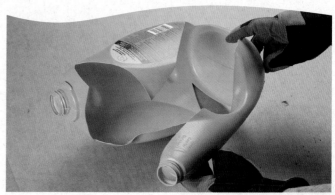

3 Determine locations for cuts by envisioning the bottle unfolding with the handle and the transom as the tail extension, the bottom panel as the abdomen, and the spigot end panel as the chest. Leave the front and back label panels attached to where you want fins on the chest area.

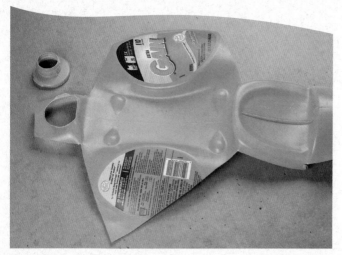

4 Cut and heat-form to fold open the bottle as described in step 3.

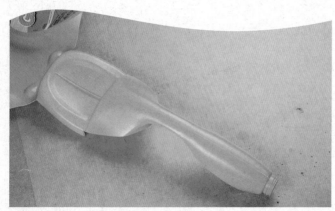

5 Trim away excess material around the end of the tail, keeping the threaded vent neck attached.

6 Remove the threaded spigot neck and make cuts to that area. Heat-form to fold open the remaining material. Note: This extension becomes the tab where you attach the head.

7 Cut away any excess perimeter material, and refine the shapes as desired.

8 Cut a tail from the top of a flattish squeeze-type bottle, keeping the threaded neck and cap intact. Dish detergent bottles are good for this.

9 Drill holes in both the vent and the tail cap, and attach the two caps back to back with a machine screw. Then, use the connected screw caps as a coupling to join the two parts together.

HEADS, GILLS, FINS, & EYES

Now it's time to give your fish a face (and a personality) by adding the head, eye, gills, and pectoral fins.

Head

1 Use a slightly convex piece of plastic that is at least as tall as the leading edge of your armature and long enough to proportionately fit your composition. I use the label panels because they have good shapes, and the label graphics add visual interest.

2 Cut the corner of the mouth so that it generally ends about one-third of the distance up from the bottom of the trailing end of the head. You can also create different facial expressions (see the basic head templates on page 136). In some situations, you may want to have a two-part head, with the lower jaw as a separate piece. In the case of a two-part head, the part that is hidden behind the head should extend enough to be attached with the eye screw so you can adjust the angle of the jaw (see the eye section, which follows).

Gills

Gills are used to define and separate the shape of the head from the body of the fish.

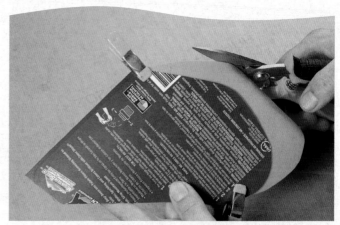

1 Hold the untrimmed piece of plastic you wish to use for the gill under the trailing edge of the finished headpiece so that it covers a minimum of ½ inch (1.3 cm) of the leading end of the gill. Tip: Use spring clips or clothespins to hold these parts in alignment.

2 Cut the trailing edge of the gill to create a tapering crescent shape, as shown.

3 Cut away any excess material that may show through the mouth or stick out above. Note: Do not cut the ½-inch (1.3 cm) hidden strip, because you will use that later to attach the gill to the armature.

Pectoral Fins

The pectoral fin can be a single piece, several spikes, or multilayered assemblies with lots of detail

1 Select plastic for the pectoral fin that is a wedge or a tapered shape, with a narrow end that will attach to the body just behind the gill and flare out toward the tail along the side of the armature.

2 Cut the piece to be at least two-thirds of the length and one-fourth of the height of the trunk of your fish body. A little extra length never hurts.

3 Detail the fin before attaching it to the armature, as it becomes more difficult to detail it once it is in place.

Eye

The eye is a key structural component of the fish piece, as the screw attaching it to the head also attaches the head to the armature and one end of the hanging wire to the piece. Because they make great eyes (and other elements), you will find that you will begin to collect all sorts and colors of plastic screw caps as you start to work with the recycled plastic.

1 Select a single soda bottle cap (or a cap of a similar size) for the eye, or nest three or more caps to make a different version of the eye. I like to offset a smaller cap in a larger one to give the effect of the eye looking in a particular direction.

2 Drill a $\frac{5}{32}$-inch (4 mm) hole through the middle of your eye selection. Tip: Cut a liner just small enough to be fitted inside the center cap, but large enough for the threads to keep it in place, if you want to cover the exposed screw end in the eye.

ASSEMBLY

Now that you have made all five parts for your fish, it's time to put them together.

1 Hold the head and gill in their proper positions against the armature, and mark where the trailing edge of the gill sits against the armature. Envision how you want to angle and position your pectoral fin along the body emerging from behind the gill. You will want to attach the pectoral fin forward of this line to hide the attachment.

2 Set the head and gill aside, and attach the pectoral fin to the armature with an electric staple gun and ½-inch (1.3 cm) staples. Note: Fold over the staple ends on the back of the piece.

3 Hold the head and gill in place against the armature, hiding the staple for the pectoral fin. Make note of the gill's position and where the trailing edge of the head lies against the gill. Note: You will want to attach the gill to the armature forward of this line to hide the staple.

6 Loosely fasten together the eye (starting with the innermost part), the head, and the armature with a 1-inch (2.5 cm) #6-32 machine screw. Put a washer on the screw before inserting, and then put another washer on the back before threading on the nut.

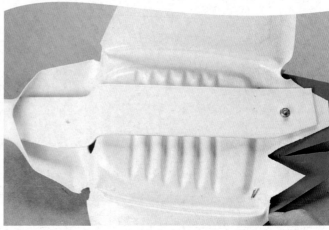

4 Set the head aside and attach the gill to the armature in the same way the pectoral fin is attached in step 2.

5 Position the largest component of the eye against the head, and drill a corresponding hole from the eye through the head. Next, positioning the head against the armature, drill a corresponding hole from the eyehole in the head through the armature.

7 Check the position of the head and eye, and make any adjustments necessary. If the piece is really floppy, add a lateral stiffening component such as an old PVC venetian blind slat.

8 Cut a piece of 12-gauge wire (copper or aluminum works best) about the length of the eye screw to the fork of the tail to make a hanger. Form an eyelet in one end of the wire to attach to the screw in the back of the eye.

9 Remove the nut from the back of the eye screw to attach the eyelet of the hanger wire, and then replace it. Tighten the nut to secure the head in place. Add a liner disk to the inner eye to hide the exposed screw, if desired.

10 Leave enough slack in the wire to make a crimp at the balance point for hanging, but first finish detailing your piece. Resolve the loose end of the hanging wire, using one of the following methods:

Make a hole in the body, hidden behind the trailing end of the pectoral fin, and pass the loose end of the hanging wire through it.

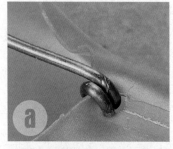

Make a hole in the back of the handle of a handletail fish, and pass the wire through to the inside of the handle (a).

Attach the trailing end of the wire to a screw in the venetian blind stiffener (b).

Glue and clamp the wire to the back of the fish (c).

Tuck the wire into the curb at the top of the body (d).

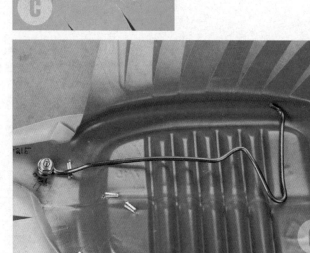

A Few More Detailing Tips

1 Cut separate fin spikes in the label panel sections that serve as the dorsal and lower fins. Cut out long, tapered slivers to create spikes. You can be really creative by using different sorts of lines, such as wavy, jagged, or perforated.

2 Refine the lines for your tail fins, and trim away anything that looks out of place.

3 Add layers of color and texture to give dimension to your pieces. I've added as many as eight different layers to the dorsal fin in same projects.

4 Attach additional layers with pop rivets.

5 Cut teeth out of an additional layer of white plastic, and attach them behind the head with the eye screw.

Marvelous
Masks

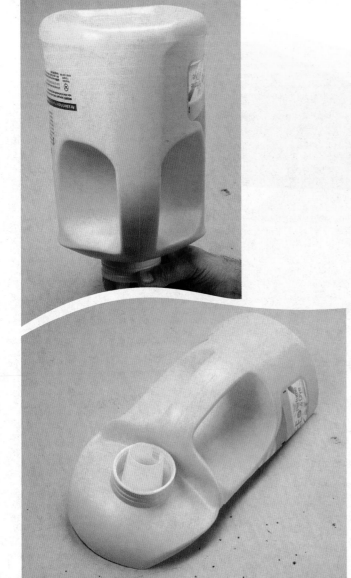

The very first piece I made from recycled plastic was a mask. If you hold almost any bottle with a handle upside down, you'll see it's the perfect base for a mask. Doesn't the connection between the transom and the cuff look like an eyebrow line, and the handle a nose? Now, get to work!

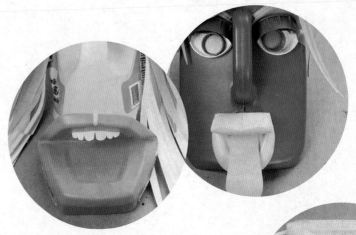

1 Cut out the handle-side section of the bottle for your mask, being sure to keep a little extra material along the edges.

2 Make the eyebrow/eye socket pieces from the lids of coffee cans or large yogurt containers.

3 Select nesting bottle caps for the eyes, and cut a portion away from the outer (largest) cap so it sits snugly under the eyebrow. Position the eyebrow/eye socket pieces, and attach them to the face through the eyes using either pop rivets or machine screws. Affix a hanging wire to the eye fasteners in the back of the piece at the same time to save a step.

4 Heat-form the mouth part of the bottle, or make a separate mouth from a coffee can lid or the bottom of a small bottle. Use the curb of the lid as the lip, and attach it with a pop rivet or glue.

5 Embellish your composition with hair, jewelry, teeth, hats, and other items to give your mask personality.

Imaginary Flora

The colors and organic shapes of most HDPE bottles sing out with potential floral designs. You can follow some of my examples, but feel free to use your own creative twists as well.

1   Cut HDPE bottle panels into petal shapes radiating out from the neck. Heat-form them open, as if peeling a banana or turning the bottle inside out. This results in a large blossom.

2   Select bottles that can be concentrically nested inside each other to make radiating flower compositions. Nest and connect the bottles through their middles with long machine screws.

3   Cut radial spikes starting from either end of colored PETE bottles, and then heat-form them to bend outward. Heat the tips to get squiggly ends.

4   Cut green PETE bottles into broad, wavy-edged strips, and then heat-form them into interesting leafy, vine-like elements for stems and foliage.

Gallery

THOMAS MCDONALD

Kozy Kannon, 2007

17 x 43 x 24 inches (43.2 x 109.2 x 61 cm)

Recycled plastic toys; assembled, screwed, glued

Photo by artist

ELISA ROBLES-CARLO

Clearly a Flower #5 (Orchid), 2008

3¾ x 3½ x ¼ inch (9.5 x 8.9 x 0.6 cm)

Glass cab, wire, recycled plastic; cut, wired, soldered

Photo by artist

CAROLIEN ADRIAANSCHE

Untitled, 2007

7⅞ x 7⅞ x 11¹³/₁₆ inches (20 x 20 x 30 cm)

Plastic detergent bottle, plastic cleaning product bottle, door handle plug; glued

Photo by Jhoeko

LISA FOO YU HSIA

Plastic Sea Crèature # 1, 2008

157 3/16 x 3 9/16 x 3 9/16 inches (400 x 9 x 9 cm)

Plastic water bottles; cut, strung

Photo by artist

BECKY CRAWFORD

Very Wiggly Necklace, 2008

Various dimensions

Detergent bottles, shampoo bottles, beach plastic, glass beads, silver, fishing line; cut

Photo by artist

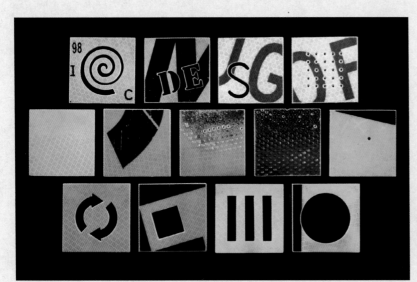

BORIS BALLY

De-Sign Series: 13 D.P.W. Brooches, 2007

2 3/16 x 2 3/16 x 1/2 inch (5.6 x 5.6 x 1.3 cm) each

Recycled aluminum traffic signs, thermoplastic resin, glass beads; hand fabricated, swaged, pierced

Photo by J.W. Johnson

Rock-n-Roll Race Car

This sci-fi dragster rattles when it rolls in a retro salute to the low-tech toys of the past. It can be fitted with a cord to become a pull toy. Using this basic concept, you can design your own dream car.

1 Cut a standard-size detergent bottle in half diagonally by starting at the shoulder edge at the top of the end panel and cutting down and around the curb at the bottom of the transom.

2 Fit the resulting handled piece with axles made from #6-32 threaded rod. Note: You will need to use several extra nuts and washers and some lock washers to adjust and secure the fit.

3 Use matching sets of larger screw caps and jar lids for the oversize rear wheels. Drill holes to assemble the wheels on the rear axle.

4 Glue two larger screw caps face to face to make the rolling, recessed center-front wheel. Put some pebbles inside the screw caps before you glue them together so they make noise when they roll.

5 Drill a pair of small screw caps for the outer front wheels. Note: These are not functional and are just for show.

6 Assemble the front axle with the recessed wheel between the outer wheels.

7 Embellish the outside with racing stripes and larger screw caps for windows, using the project photo as an inspiration.

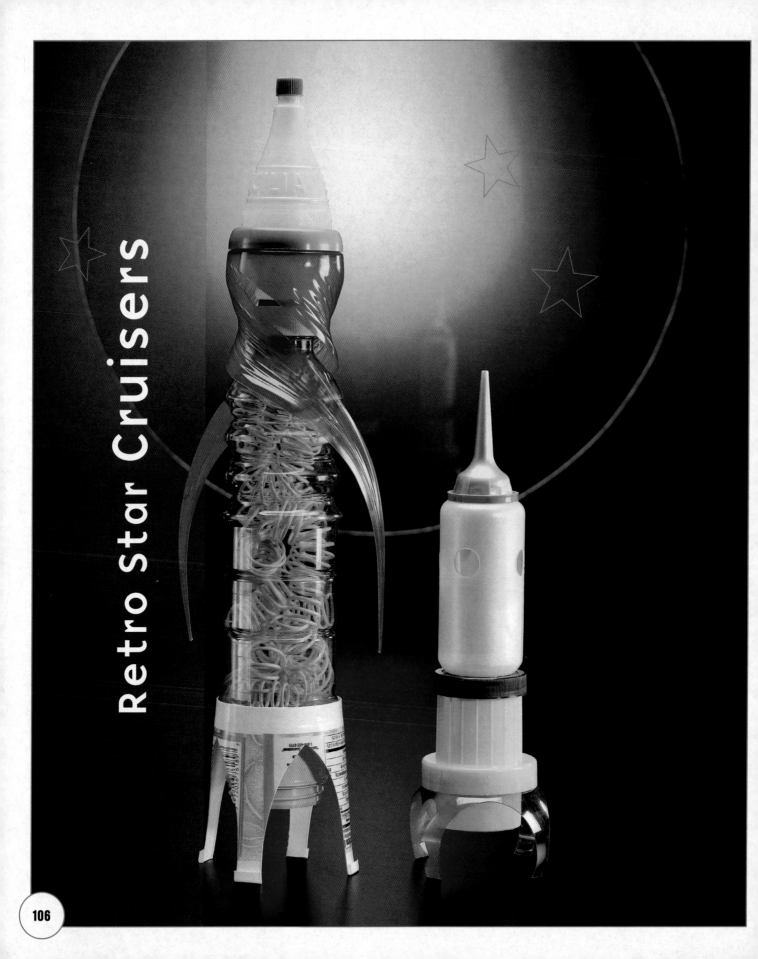

Retro Star Cruisers

These gizmos that Buck Rogers or Chewbacca would be right at home piloting are jet-propelled by your imagination. Unusual bottle and cap shapes from condiment, cosmetic, and sport-drink containers are the perfect materials for your creative journey to boldly go where no man has gone before.

1 Drill and screw stacked bottles or caps together using machine screws. Note: You can often screw the bottom of one bottle to the top of the next bottle, using the cap as a coupling.

2 Cut legged stanchions from dairy product tubs or bottle end sections. Attach with machine screws or glue. Don't overestimate the strength of plastics. Keep the legs stout.

3 Sandwich different-colored caps and breakaway cap seal rings between layers to add visual interest.

4 Cut portholes with Forstner drill bits. Place strips of colored PETE inside holes for windowpanes.

5 Attach detergent-bottle measuring caps with machine screws to create rocket engines.

6 Cut streamlined, symmetrical components made from colored PETE elements for futuristic fins. Glue them onto the rocket.

An Ace of an Aeroplane

1 Select a 150-ounce (4.5 L) bottle with a long handle. Visualize a propeller where the spout for the spigot is attached and a tail extension of the airplane out of the handle section with the vent spout.

2 Cut across the shoulder between the spouts and down along the edges between the label panels and the cuff section. Continue the cut to the curb at a point about halfway between each end of the bottom panel.

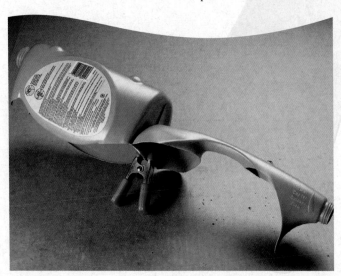

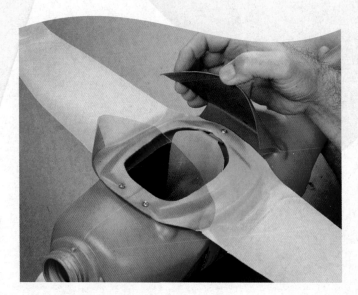

3 Heat-form the bottom panel between the ends of the previous cuts, and fold the bottle open 180° to establish the basic fuselage armature.

4 Trim away the cuff and any excess material around the vent spout. Leave the vent spout and threads intact and attached, and keep some material for the tail skid, as shown. Note: Use a large spring clip to hold the fuselage pieces in place while you continue working on other parts of the project.

5 Select a tall, flat-sided bottle for the wings. Cut away the handle side, shoulder, neck, and end panel, leaving the front and back label panels connected by the bottom panel.

6 Heat-form the wings open along the curb lines. Massage the heated wing shapes with gloved hands until they are cooled and set. Trim the wings as desired.

7 Cut the end-panel section from the scrap left from making the wings in step 5. Heat-form and fold the piece in half. Fit the top portion under the trailing edge of the wings to form the back of the cockpit, as shown.

8 Position the wings on top of the fuselage. Draw and cut out a cockpit hole in the bridge between the wings. Note: Be sure to keep enough of the bridge between the wings intact to assure structural integrity. Trim the bottom edge of the end panel piece from step 7 to match the trailing edge of the cockpit.

9 Draw and cut a matching cockpit hole through the top of the fuselage.

10 Cut a curved section of colored PETE plastic, making a wide folded tab in the middle of the bottom for the windshield, as shown.

11 Drill holes in the leading edge of the bridge between the wings. Make matching holes in the windshield tabs and fuselage for mounting the wings and the windshield at the front of the cockpit.

12 Repeat step 11 for the trailing edge of the wing bridge, including holes to attach the end panel piece from step 7. Set these various parts aside.

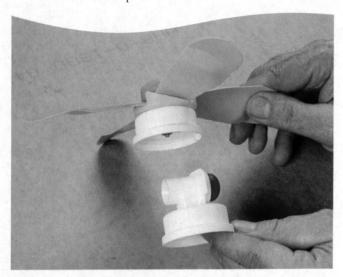

13 Cut the propeller out of the thicker bottom panel from a large bottle, as shown. Heat the propeller blades to soften, and twist them to a pitched angle.

14 Saw the spigot part off of the spigot screw cap. Cut a spiral-stepped screw cap to hold the propeller angles in place, as shown. Use the base of the spigot cap for mounting the propeller onto the fuselage, using a 2-inch (5 cm) #6-32 machine screw. You will need several nuts, washers, and lock washers to make this assembly. Set the assembly aside.

15 Cut a folded label panel to make the tail fin.

16 Cut a pair of connected tail wings from an end panel.

17 Cut slots to fit the tail fin and tail wings into the area just below the neck of the vent spout, as shown. Be sure to keep the threads for the vent spout intact so you can use the screw cap to hold the tail fin and wings in place.

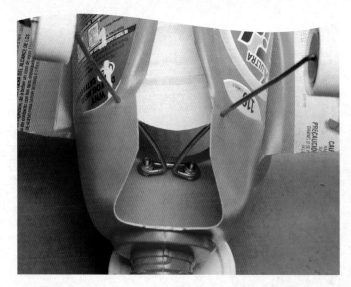

18 Heat-form the tail skid and assemble the tail section, as shown.

19 Cut away the bottom panel connected to the front section of the fuselage, and heat-form the sides to wrap the label panels under, narrowing and streamlining the overall shape.

20 Loosely attach the wings, the windshield, and the back of the cockpit to the front section of the fuselage, using #6-32 machine screws.

21 Bend the landing-gear legs out of 8-gauge copper wire, and attach them to the bottom of the windshield screws through the front of the fuselage, as shown.

22 Drill holes in two pairs of face-to-face nesting screw caps for the wheels. Attach each set to the landing gear legs using cap nuts. You can find self-tapping cap nuts in most hardware stores.

23 Attach the propeller assembly to the front section of the fuselage, and tighten all the fasteners in the wing assembly.

24 Attach the front and tail fuselage pieces together with pop rivets by slipping the tail-section end panel inside the open end at the rear of the front section. Carefully align the components before attaching the pieces.

Make 'Em Mobile

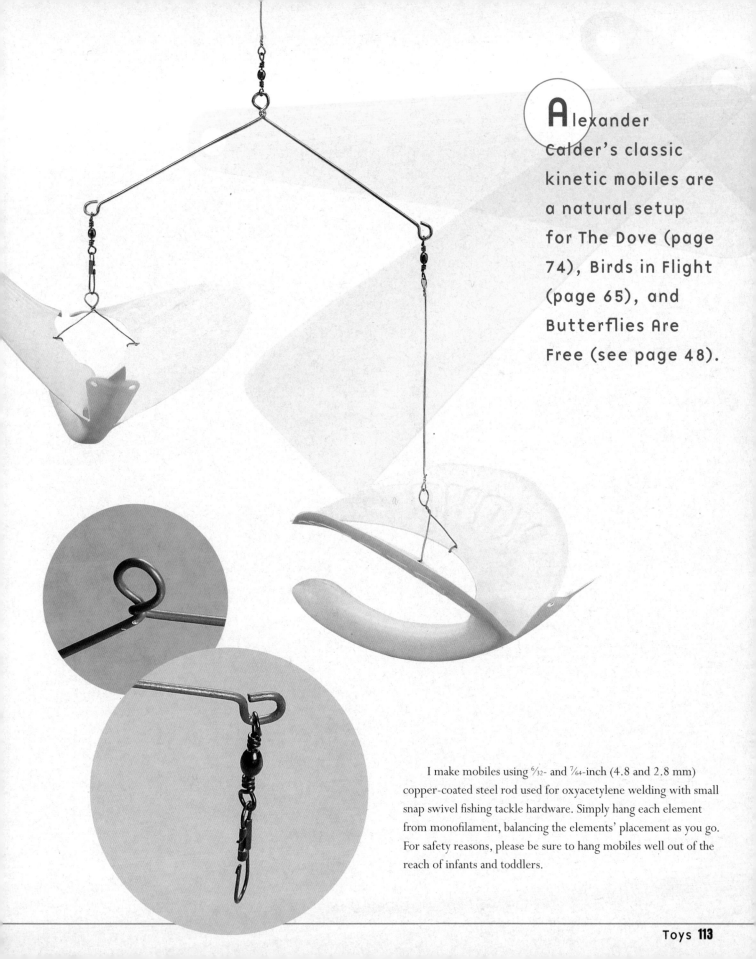

Alexander Calder's classic kinetic mobiles are a natural setup for The Dove (page 74), Birds in Flight (page 65), and Butterflies Are Free (see page 48).

I make mobiles using ⁶⁄₃₂- and ⁷⁄₆₄-inch (4.8 and 2.8 mm) copper-coated steel rod used for oxyacetylene welding with small snap swivel fishing tackle hardware. Simply hang each element from monofilament, balancing the elements' placement as you go. For safety reasons, please be sure to hang mobiles well out of the reach of infants and toddlers.

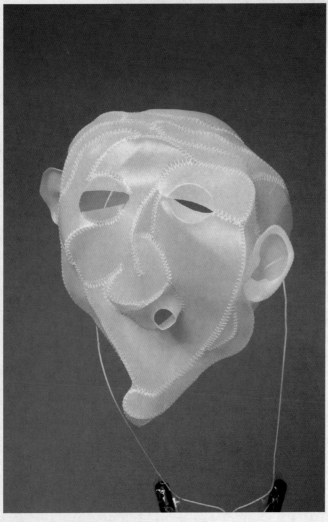

ELIZABETH WINTRISS-MOORE

Rip Van Winkle Mask, 2004

11¹³⁄₁₆ x 10¹⁄₄ x 5⁷⁄₈ inches (30 x 26 x 15 cm)

Plastic milk jug upholstery thread; sewn, cut

Photo by Karen Kirchhoff

ELIZABETH WINTRISS-MOORE

Dumpster Demon (Nightmare at the Video Store), 2003

72 x 24 x 12 inches (182.9 x 61 x 30.5 cm)

Dry cleaning bags, video tape, CDs, juice bottles, bicycle inner tubes, milk jugs, window screen, vinyl tubing; crocheted, cut, glued

Photo by Karen Kirchhoff

LIAUNG CHUNG YEN

Changeability #4, 2007

3¹⁵⁄₁₆ x 5¹⁄₂ x 5¹⁄₂ inches (10 x 14 x 14 cm)

Recycled plastic water bottle and cap, rubber; cut, tied

Photo by artist

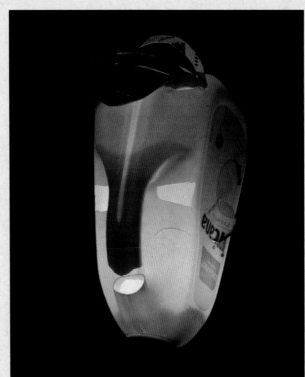

PHIL GOLDBERG

Trishda, 2008

6 x 10 inches (15.2 x 25.4 cm)

Recycled juice container; cut, sliced, tabbed

Photos by artist

MICHELLE STITZLEIN

Cappy Holidays Wreath, 2005

36 x 23 x 12 inches (91.4 x 58.4 x 30.5 cm)

Recycled plastic bottle caps, wire; strung

Photo by artist

Groovy Jellyfish Lamp

This marine-fantasy mood lighting will take you back to the daze of free love and purple haze. You'll need a candelabra-base light kit to give your lamp a glow. Use a small wattage bulb, or all your hard work could potentially melt or distort.

1 Select a jug-type detergent bottle, preferably from translucent material. Remove the pouring spout, leaving the screw threads intact.

2 Remove the bottom of the bottle, and cut a tentacle-like pattern along the sides of the remaining portion of the bottle.

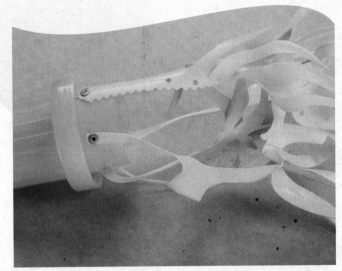

3 Drill a ¹³⁄₃₂-inch (1 cm) hole in the center of the screw-on top. Surround this hole with a pattern of five to six ⅛-inch (3 mm) holes to provide ventilation for the heat created by the light bulb.

4 Cut some accent tentacles from an alternative color, and attach them to the inner lip of the screw-on top with pop rivets. Note: Place the pop rivets so that you can still put the cap back on the bottle.

5 Install the electric lighting parts for a candelabra-base light socket inside the screw-on top according to the directions that come with the kit. Wire it so that the lamp cord comes out the top.

6 Feed the tentacle ends of the screw-on top assembly into the top of the main bottle, and screw the assembly in place. As an alternative to using the threads for a screw-on top, you can glue the parts together.

Here's a contemporary design easily made from different colored screw-on measuring caps from detergent bottles and a tubular electric LED light cord, available at most building centers.

1 You will need about four to five caps per foot of LED light cord. Use a Forstner drill bit slightly larger than the diameter of the light cord to drill out the center of your caps.

2 String the caps together with an LED light cord. No need to glue them at all.

3 You could also experiment with tiny holiday twinkle lights—perhaps using the measuring caps as shades? As a general rule, if a bulb gets too hot to hold in your closed hand for a minute, it's too hot for plastic!

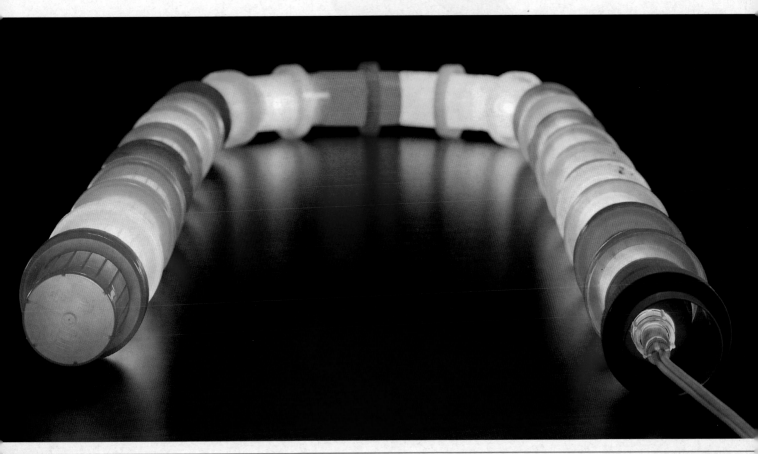

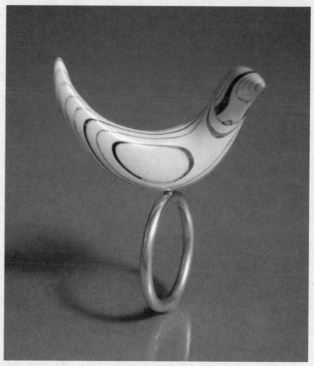

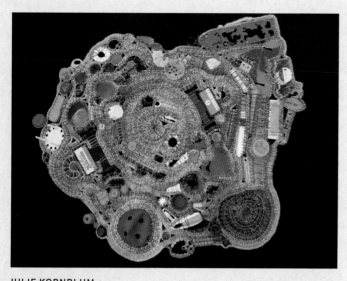

JULIE KORNBLUM
Gyre, 2008
24 x 18 x 2 inches (61 x 45.7 x 5.1 cm)
Wool, waxed linen, plastic discards, toys; coiled
Photo by artist

TABITHA OTT
Untitled, 2007
2 x 1 x 1 inch (5.1 x 2.5 x 2.5 cm) each
Recycled plastic gift cards, reclaimed silver; laminated, carved, polished, cast, drawn
Photo by artist

MICHAEL DIEGO BYRNES
Stroll, 2008
12 x 9 x 44 inches (30.5 x 22.9 x 111.8 cm)
Recycled bottles, caps, and spouts, screws, bolts
Photo by Steve Loar

VICKIE JO FRANKS

Yellow Creek Cat Composed in Blue, 2007

11 3/8 x 13 x 3/8 inch (28.9 x 33 x 1 cm)

Plastic bag, plastic lid, cloth fragments, thumb tacks, gift bag handles; hand stitched, crocheted, glued

Photo by Hickory Museum of Art

2ROSES

Big Red Plastic Bracelet, 2007

4 inches (10.2 cm) in diameter

Recycled water bottle caps, copper, sterling silver; die cut, hammer set

Photo by Corliss Rose

HARMONY RITCHIE

Great Blue Heron, 2007

29 x 23 x 5 inches (73.7 x 58.4 x 12.7 cm)

Recycled plastic, screws, wire, cardboard; heat shaped, riveted, screwed

Photo by Steve Loar

ANETTE KITHIER
Medusa, 2000
9¹³/₁₆ x 11¹³/₁₆ x 11¹³/₁₆ inches (25 x 30 x 30 cm)
Recycled plastic bottle; cut

Photo by artist

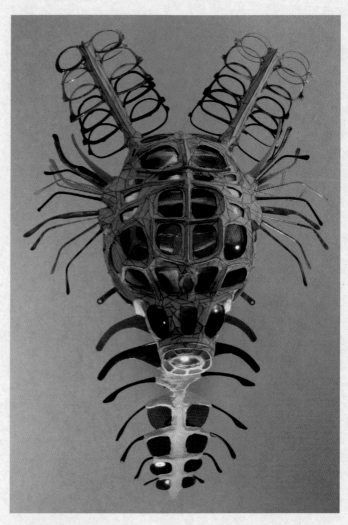

CHRISTOPHER MCMANUS
Space Mask, 2008
30 x 20 x 10 inches (76.2 x 50.8 x 25.4 cm)
Plastic sunglasses, acrylic paint; paper maché
constructed

Photo by artist

BARBARA SCHNEIDER

Bender's Plus Promotion Bag, 2005

11 x 24³/₈ x 2³/₄ inches (28 x 62 x 7 cm)

Bag; image transfer, sewn, appliqué

Photos by artist

Afterword

For well more than a century, Americans have been turning discards into useful and beautiful new things. Whose family doesn't treasure a quilt, or a rag rug, made from scraps of family clothing? Certainly our pioneer forefathers and mothers made do by reusing precious resources, converting them into the new. We may not always recognize their efforts as art, but we have clearly rediscovered their creativity to conceive the new from the old. Artists, famous or not, have been recycling trash for years. Alexander Calder made sculptural toys from colorful coffee cans. Louise Nevelson sanded wooden shoe trees and hat-blocking forms to neutralize them, and then composed them into wall assemblages. Mark di Suvero and John Chamberlain both recycled steel into large-scale sculptures. And Joseph Cornell created boxed poetry from discards.

In our bounty of the present, America leads the world in throwing away what previous generations found ways to use again, refashion, or remake into something entirely different. Though many communities have successful programs of recycling reusable trash to keep it out of landfills, we lag behind the rest of the world in reducing post-consumer trash. Today we readily recycle paper, glass, and several metals, but plastics remain a thorny problem. We recycle only five percent of all the plastics produced in this country.

Plastics have been used in the arts for at least 70 years. In the 1930s, weavers began to experiment with plastic threads and yarns. By the 1960s, jewelers were exploiting plastic possibilities by making pendants and bracelets that were lightweight and colorful. And in the 1970s, furniture makers began to embellish wood with colorful inlays of plastic resins. So it was only a matter of time until artists began to explore the pliable, colorful variety of plastic materials that are readily available as discards to make art—just as past generations used scraps of fabric or tin cans.

In my 1998 book and exhibition, *Trashformations: Recycled Materials in Contemporary American Art and Design*, I included garments made from plastic six-pack rings, a quilt composed of colorful detergent-bottle plastic, and baskets woven from plastic bread wrappers and strapping from bales of newspapers. Then I discovered the remarkable David Edgar and his Plastiquarium with a variety of tropical fish to rival nature, but made from recycled plastic bottles. Edgar's colorful fish, seen singly or in schools that can animate an entire wall, bring new energy to recycled plastic art. Other sea creatures, or masks, utilize not only the focus-group approved colors intended to catch our attention on supermarket shelves, but often incorporate the actual shape of a bottle's handle into the new composition. Just as Andy Warhol validated commercial consumer products in the Pop Art movement of the 1960s, Edgar takes it a step further. These new sculptures, informed by the years he worked in steel, don't obliterate their origins on supermarket shelves, but give viewers an "aha" moment of recognition after smiling at Edgar's reconceptualization of a familiar material.

Folk artists the world over have been making do with discards for decades—even centuries. But Edgar's plastic creatures will not be confused with the work of makers uneducated in the arts. He brings not only the academic discipline of the professor of art that he has been for years, but a sound knowledge of the outsider or visionary artist inspired primarily by material possibilities. He has not only the creative vision, but the depth of experience in all of the visual arts to assemble this remarkable new look at plastics in art.

Lloyd E. Herman
Director Emeritus, Renwick Gallery of the
Smithsonian American Art Museum

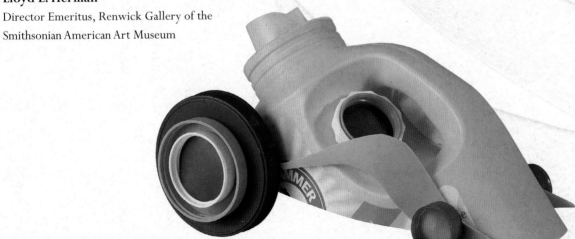

Templates

Use the following templates as guides to create your own versions of the projects.

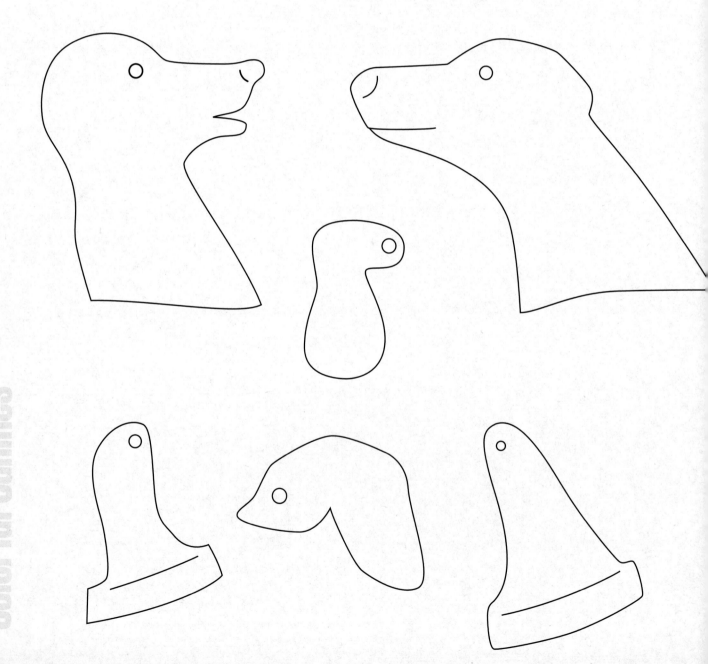

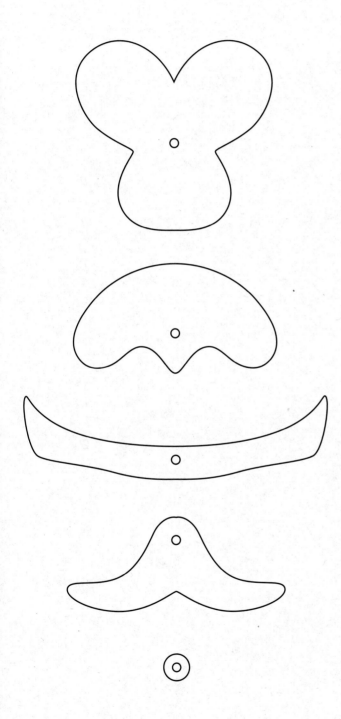

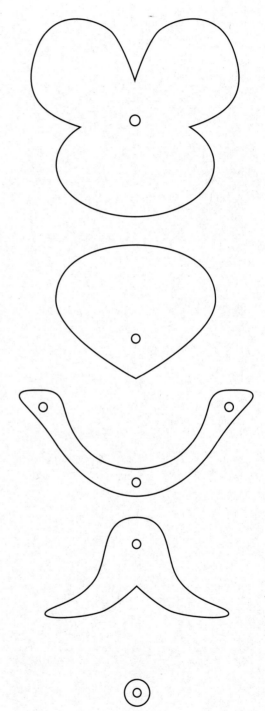

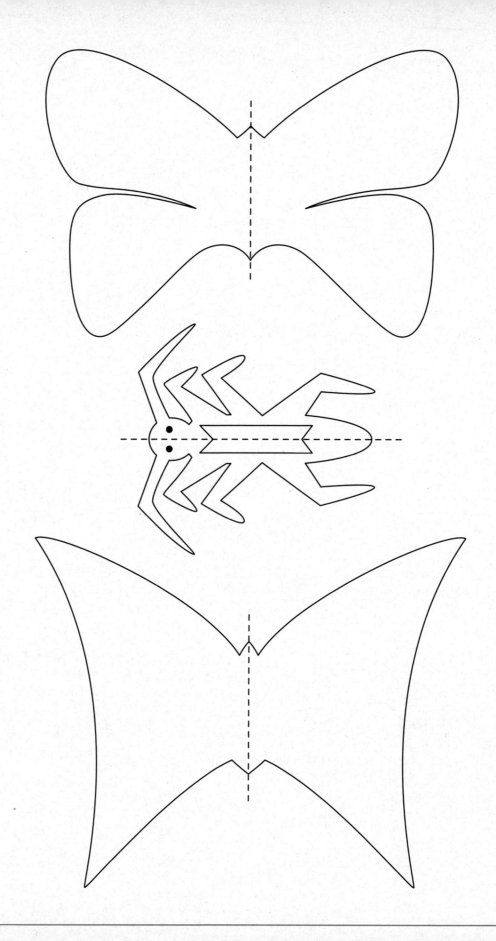

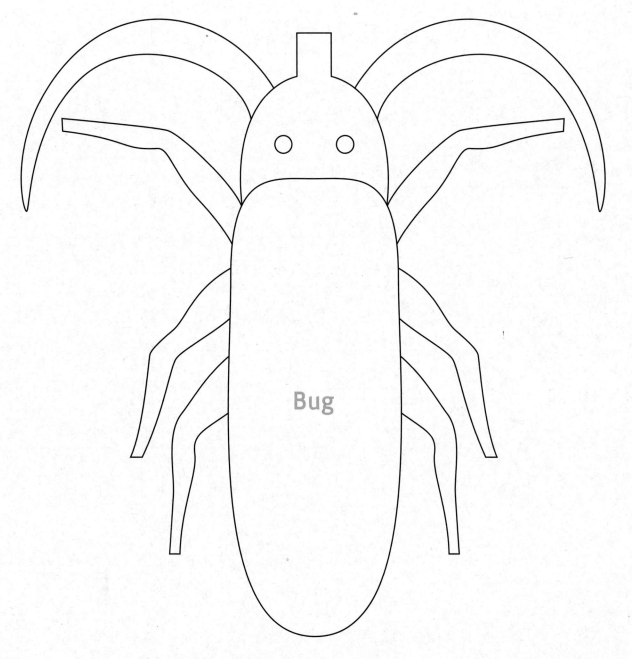

Bug

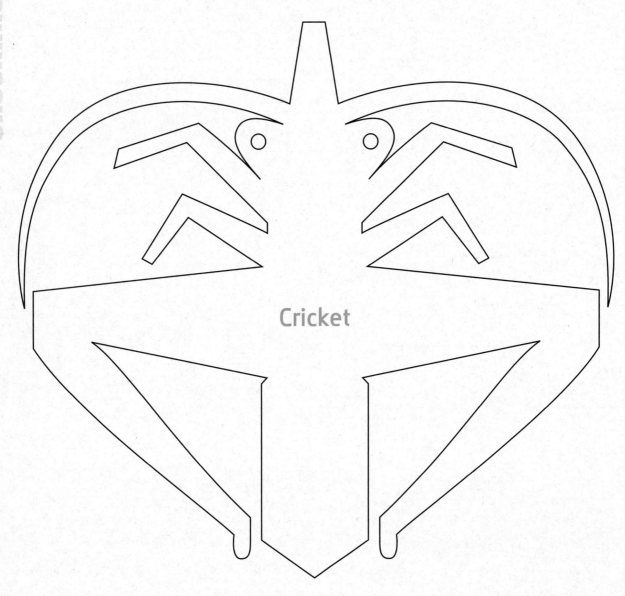

Cricket

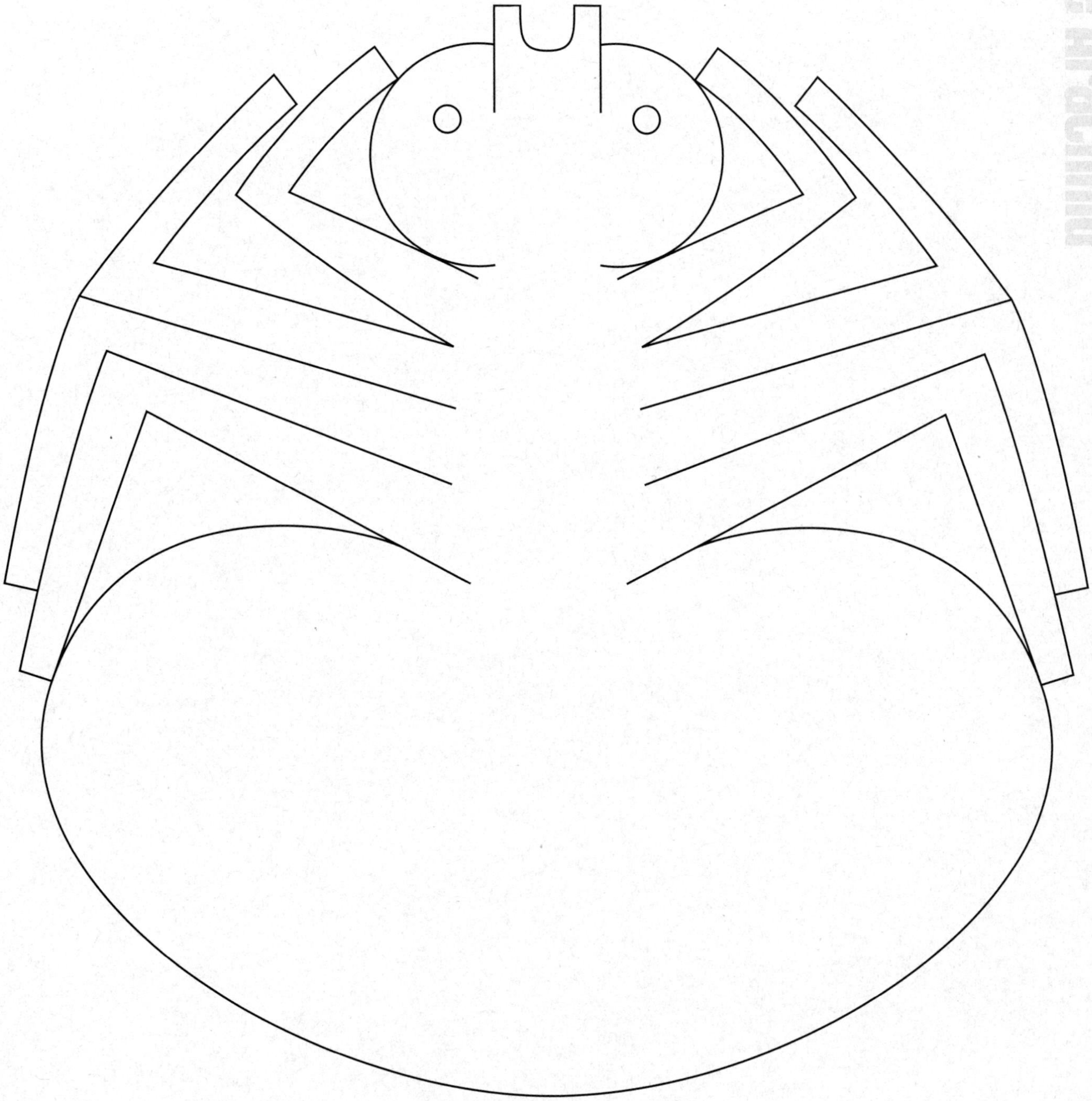

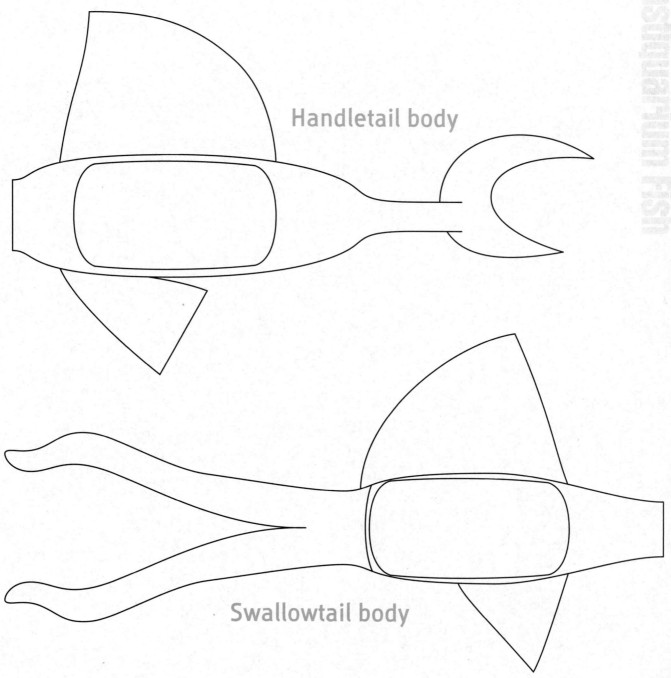

Handletail body

Swallowtail body

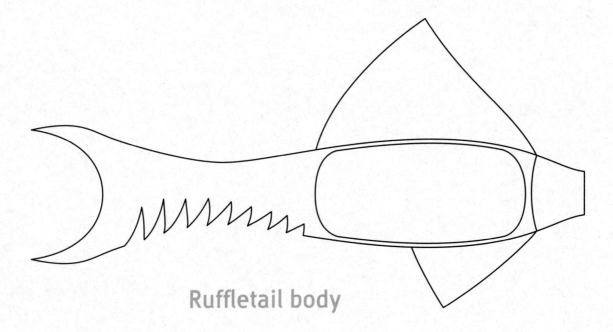

Ruffletail body

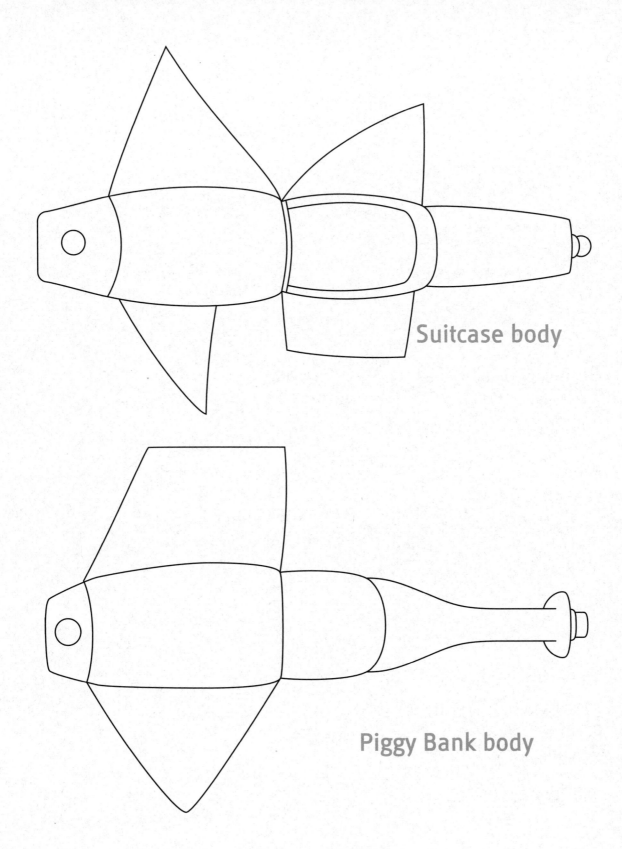

Suitcase body

Piggy Bank body

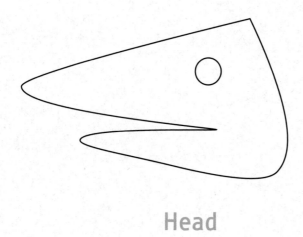

Head

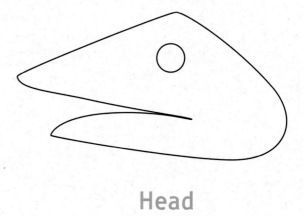

Head

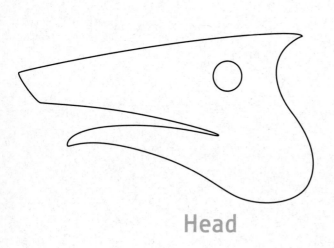

Head

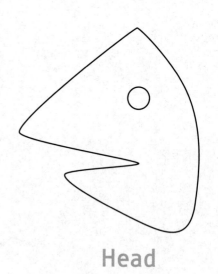

Head

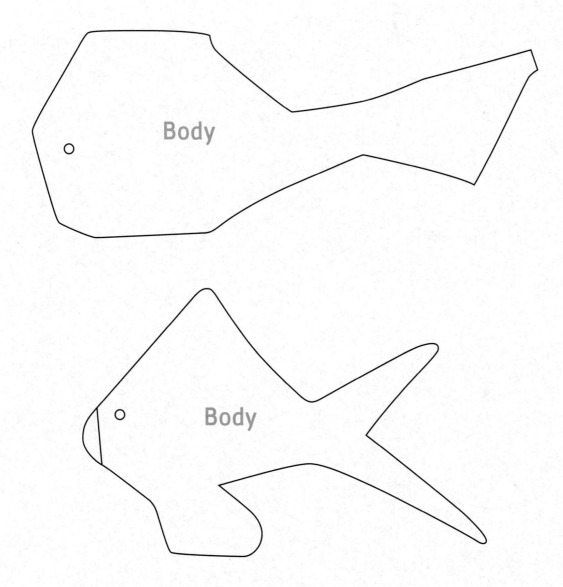

Body

Body

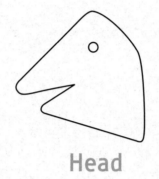

Head

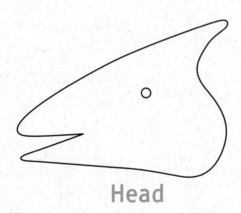

Head

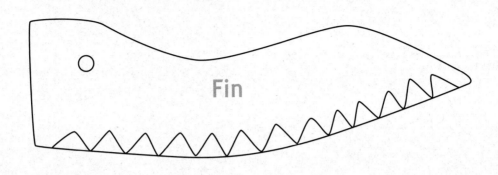

Fin

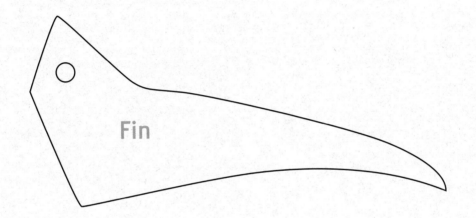

Fin

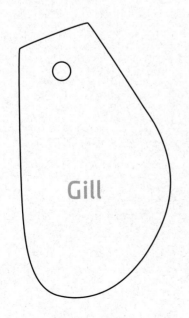

Gill

Gill

David Edgar, inventor of the Plastiquarium, is a third-generation Floridian now living in North Carolina with his wife, Robin. An MFA graduate in sculpture from Cranbrook Academy of Art in Bloomfield Hills, Michigan, he also holds a BFA in sculpture from the Minneapolis College of Art and Design. A former arts administrator and associate professor of art, he is credited with the development of both the Crealde School of Art and the Armory Art Center, both in Florida. He also worked as a production artist on the EPCOT Center and Tokyo Disneyland projects for the Imagineering division of the Walt Disney Company. A full-time artist today, Edgar's exhibition history reflects over 30 years of consistent activity, and his artwork is represented internationally in corporate, institutional, and private collections.

Robin A. Edgar, namer of the Plastiquarium, writes profiles, art reviews, and features for national, regional, and local publications. She travels throughout the United States as a keynote speaker and workshops facilitator, teaching reminiscence-writing techniques based on her two books, *In My Mother's Kitchen: An Introduction to the Healing Power of Reminiscence* and *Personal Legacies: Surviving the Great Depression.* After many years of helping David schlep his steel work around, she is delighted that he is so successful with the lighter medium of recycled plastic.

Every artist has their muse. I am so thankful for my wife, Robin, who miraculously continues to tolerate my eccentricities and support my creative dreams. She also gave the Plastiquarium its name and co-authored this book.

Every artist has their teachers. I am indebted to Mary Purser, who set me on an artistic path early on. Lucien Lavioe opened my eyes to an egalitarian view of the creative experience. Jere Lykins did not give up on me. Ron Wilczek embraced me as an equal. Cork Marcheschi helped me to break out of the ordinary. Michael Hall dispelled my egocentric tendencies and introduced me to the world of folk art.

Every artist has their supporters. Lloyd Herman first supported Plastiquarium as a curator and then wrote a wonderful essay for this book. McColl Center for Visual Art offered me an affiliate residency during which I realized the Plastiquarium's potential. The Wildacres Retreat Center awarded me a summer residency where Robin and I developed the proposal for this book. The Charlotte Mecklenburg Art and Sciences Council awarded me an artist project grant that helped to develop the projects for this book. Bruce Gledhill sanctioned an exhibition of the Plastiquarium and the on-site photography at the Mecklenburg County Recycling Center for some of the images on these pages.

Lastly, this book was made possible with the support of the Lark Books team. It could not have happened without the sage advice of Terry Taylor, our editor; Kristi Pfeffer, the art director (and cheerleader); and Steve Mann, the talented photographer.

acknowledgments

2Roses
Anaheim, California

Adriaansche, Carolien
WG Den Haag,
Netherlands

Bally, Boris
Providence, Rhode
Island

Boulay, Diana
Brownsburg-Chatam,
Quebec, Canada

Bradford, Robert
Cornwall, England

Byrnes, Michael Diego
Ebensburg,
Pennsylvania

Calderwood, Sofia
Peninsula, Ohio

Chung Yen, Liaung
Henrietta, New York

Conover-Loar, Kim
Indiana, Pennsylvania

Crawford, Becky
Red Ruth, Cornwall,
United Kingdom

Dahari, Anat
Tel-Aviv, Israel

Dahlsen, John
Byron Bay, New South
Wales, Australia

Dillon, Marge
Junction City, Oregon

Franks, Vickie Jo
Shelby, North Carolina

Geltman, Elizabeth
Glass
Washington, DC

Geltman, Rachel
Washington, DC

Gilbson, Adam
Tel-Aviv, Israel

Goldberg, Phil
Ridgefield, Connecticut

Hotaling, Roxanne N.
Manchester,
Pennsylvania

Hsia, Lisa Foo Yu
Selan Gor Darul Ehsan,
Malaysia

Hsiao, Chia-Pei
Kaohsiung City, Taiwan

Karhu, Minna
Lapeenranta, Finland

Kithier, Anette
Dusseldorf, Germany

Kornblum, Julie
Woodland Hills,
California

Matsree, Yonatan
Tel-Aviv, Israel

McCartney, Edward Lane
Houston, Texas

McDonald, Thomas
Oak Park, Illinois

McManus, Christopher
Seattle, Washington

Nash, Heath
Cape Town, South Africa

Ott, Tabitha
Saint Matthews, South
Carolina

Reifenberg, Dodi
Berlin, Germany

Richards, John, D.
Burnsville, North
Carolina

Ritchie, Harmony
Smichkburg,
Pennsylvania

Robles-Carlo, Elisa
Pen Argyl, Pennsylvania

Saito, Yuka
New York, New York

Sales, Michelle
Winfield, Illinois

Schneider, Barbara
Rochum, Germany

Shuttleworth, Lana
Echo Park, California

Stange, Greg
Worthington, Ohio

Stitzlein, Michelle
Baltimore

Wagner, Leigh
Brisbane, Queensland,
Australia

Wald, Jon
Charlotte, North Carolina

Weber, Ginelle
Port Orford, Oregon

Wintriss-Moore,
Elizabeth
Haddenfield, New Jersey

Go Make Some